5-Star Review by ~~Readers~~ ~~Favorite~~

HR Analytics Essentials You Always Wanted to Know by Dr. Michael J. Walsh is an intellectually fascinating blend of instruction, theory, and illustrative samples. Human Resource professionals like myself are deeply rooted in the modern-day blend of people-centric practices supported by analytical data. This guidebook expertly walks readers through the more foundational principles of the analytical process and is packed with HR-specific conditions and steadily deepens the discussion from foundational to more advanced topics. Individuals with a basic background in statistics will quickly absorb the contents and those with experience in HR will easily identify opportunities for utilization. This book could also pique the interest of Organizational Change Management professionals and anyone interested in organizational strategy. My personal favorite chapter was on job analysis.

Dr. Michael J. Walsh clearly understands his audience and steadily walks the reader through familiar terminology, grasping the goals of modern HR professionals to add quantifiable contributions to their organizations. The content is delivered concisely and flows through the various concepts presented with ease. Through each new chapter, I found myself thinking back to the author's emphasis on Organizational Readiness and how truly important it is to gauge and expand with intention. What we HR pros wouldn't give to be organizationally prepared to dive into the critical analyses outlined in HR Analytics Essentials You Always Wanted to Know! This guidebook will have HR practitioners itching to get started, and ready to dive into the various scenarios. I highly recommend readers pick this one up and keep it on your desk for quick reference.

This review is for an earlier edition.

SELF-LEARNING MANAGEMENT SERIES

TITLE	PAPERBACK* ISBN
ACCOUNTING, FINANCE & ECONOMICS	
COST ACCOUNTING AND MANAGEMENT ESSENTIALS	9781636511030
FINANCIAL ACCOUNTING ESSENTIALS	9781636510972
FINANCIAL MANAGEMENT ESSENTIALS	9781636511009
MACROECONOMICS ESSENTIALS	9781636511818
MICROECONOMICS ESSENTIALS	9781636511153
PERSONAL FINANCE ESSENTIALS	9781636511849
ENTREPRENEURSHIP & STRATEGY	
BUSINESS PLAN ESSENTIALS	9781636511214
BUSINESS STRATEGY ESSENTIALS	9781949395778
ENTREPRENEURSHIP ESSENTIALS	9781636511603
GENERAL MANAGEMENT	
BUSINESS LAW ESSENTIALS	9781636511702
DECISION MAKING ESSENTIALS	9781636510026
LEADERSHIP ESSENTIALS	9781636510316
PRINCIPLES OF MANAGEMENT ESSENTIALS	9781636511542
TIME MANAGEMENT ESSENTIALS	9781636511665

*Also available in Hardback & Ebook formats

SELF-LEARNING MANAGEMENT SERIES

TITLE	PAPERBACK* ISBN

HUMAN RESOURCE MANAGEMENT

Title	ISBN
DIVERSITY IN THE WORKPLACE ESSENTIALS	9781636511122
HR ANALYTICS ESSENTIALS	9781636510347
HUMAN RESOURCE MANAGEMENT ESSENTIALS	9781949395839
ORGANIZATIONAL BEHAVIOR ESSENTIALS	9781636510378
ORGANIZATIONAL DEVELOPMENT ESSENTIALS	9781636511481

MARKETING & SALES MANAGEMENT

Title	ISBN
DIGITAL MARKETING ESSENTIALS	9781949395747
MARKETING MANAGEMENT ESSENTIALS	9781636511788
SALES MANAGEMENT ESSENTIALS	9781636510743
SERVICES MARKETING ESSENTIALS	9781636511733

OPERATIONS & PROJECT MANAGEMENT

Title	ISBN
AGILE ESSENTIALS	9781636510057
OPERATIONS & SUPPLY CHAIN MANAGEMENT ESSENTIALS	9781949395242
PROJECT MANAGEMENT ESSENTIALS	9781636510712
STAKEHOLDER ENGAGEMENT ESSENTIALS	9781636511511

*Also available in Hardback & Ebook formats

This page is intentionally left blank

SELF-LEARNING MANAGEMENT SERIES

HR ANALYTICS ESSENTIALS

YOU ALWAYS WANTED TO KNOW

MICHAEL J. WALSH, PhD

HR Analytics Essentials

You Always Wanted To Know

Paperback ISBN 10: 1-63651-034-5
Paperback ISBN 13: 978-1-63651-034-7

Ebook ISBN 10: 1-63651-035-3
Ebook ISBN 13: 978-1-63651-035-4

Hardback ISBN 10: 1-63651-036-1
Hardback ISBN 13: 978-1-63651-036-1

Library of Congress Control Number: 2021930400

This publication is designed to provide accurate and authoritative information in regard to the subject matter covered. The Author has made every effort in the preparation of this book to ensure the accuracy of the information. However, information in this book is sold without warranty either expressed or implied. The Author or the Publisher will not be liable for any damages caused or alleged to be caused either directly or indirectly by this book.

Vibrant Publishers books are available at special quantity discount for sales promotions, or for use in corporate training programs. For more information please write to bulkorders@vibrantpublishers.com

Please email feedback / corrections (technical, grammatical or spelling) to spellerrors@vibrantpublishers.com

To access the complete catalogue of Vibrant Publishers, visit www.vibrantpublishers.com

What experts say about this book!

Michael J. Walsh's book does much more than just study the qualitative themes of storytelling. HR Analytics actually combines qualitative and quantitative storytelling practices, and applies the nexus to recruiting, staffing, training, and communicating. HR Analytics relates to my field of storytelling by skillfully pulling together both the qualitative and the quantitative patterns, then composing an integrative, succinct story the organization is ready to embrace. A crucial step is determining how best to display the story with qualitative data and if needed, a statistical analysis of demographics. So, what is the benefit of combining hard core analytics with good storytelling practices? First, HR Analytics combines ways to tell the story, to manage expectations, track the process, and enact possibilities for improvement. Second, it combines organizational network diagnosis of how people are communicating with one another with ways by creating a process of recommendations for change management that improves long term organizational readiness. Finally, once people understand the basic analytic techniques, telling a story to different demographic audiences can bring the right candidates that fit what the organization is all about.

– David M. Boje,

Professor Aalborg University, Denmark;

Emeritus Professor New Mexico State University.

Every function of an organization can benefit from analytics. Dr. Michael Walsh has and his book 'HR Analytics Essentials' provides a helpful framework for establishing and using analytics to support the Human Resources function and key decision-making. This book is a good tool for individuals in the field of H.R. and managers.

– Leslie Yerkes

President Catalyst Consulting Group, Inc.

What experts say about this book!

This book provides a good, basic overview of HR analytics that is easy to understand and is not overly technical. It could be a useful supplement to an introduction to HR text used in an undergraduate class to provide additional coverage of HR analytics which is especially important to the strategic role of HR in organizations.

> **– Loren Kuzuhara**
> **Teaching Professor Department of Management and Human Resources**
> **University of Wisconsin-Madison**

This book explains the scientific method of inquiry as it is applied to HR functions in a clear and understandable manner. The book has easily viewed charts, graphs, case studies, discussions questions, and quizzes to help the reader. The use of statistics to operationalize data is easy to comprehend. The book covers the essential areas of the HR function in organizations such as staffing and training and compensating both salaried and hourly employees. A plus are the video tutorials available online. I would recommend this book without reservation to both, teachers, students or practitioner of HR who wish to comprehend the subject matter of HR Analytics.

> **– Jerry Spiegel PhD**
> **Adjunct Professor, United States University & Co-Director,**
> **Global Health Research Program**

What experts say about this book!

HR Analytics Essentials is a competent source for those wanting a primer on using data about people to drive meaningful change within an organization. While most textbooks in this area focus on either quantitative analysis or psychological theory, Dr. Walsh's work does an effective job at bridging the gap between these two through an organizational lens. By exposing the reader to a broad range of important concepts relevant to HR analytics, this book is a terrific starting point for those wanting a framework to understand both the importance and application of data in human resources.

– James Meersman

Assistant Professor, Juniata College

No matter where you turn, there is pressure to create more value with data. Human Resources is no different. In his book "HR Analytics Essentials", Dr. Michael Walsh highlights how best to leverage data and analytics to address critical people-related questions. He outlines a pragmatic approach to HR Analytics for the most novice to the most advanced. His writing style is easy to follow, and often funny, without talking down to the reader. The book covers an enormous amount of ground in a condensed way. This book is a great resource for HR generalists and HR analytic professionals.

– Wendy Hirsch, PhD

VP HR Technology, Analytics, & Services, Eaton.

What experts say about this book!

Workforce analytics and metric are changing the employment landscape, and HR professionals who embrace data analytics as they examine employee behaviors and preferences have a great opportunity to improve productivity in the workplace. HR Analytics Essentials is must read for every human resource professional and the book itself is a must have in human resource's toolbox. If you want to move from being analytically resistant to analytically willing and finally become analytically savvy you must start with this book first.

– Fernán R. Cepero, MA, MS, PHR, SHRM-CP,

Organizational & Global Leader Senior Human Resources Business Partner

YMCA of Greater Rochester - Association Office

About the Author

 Dr. Michael Walsh is an industrial and organizational psychologist with over 15 years of human resources and people analytics experience. Michael currently leads Global Talent Management and Organizational Effectiveness for Eaton Corporation's Vehicle Group. He also teaches a Human Resources Analytics course for master's level students at the University of Illinois and Wayne State University. Previously, Michael's passion for People Analytics landed him at Bloomberg and Fiat Chrysler Automobiles where he started and led the Global People Strategy and Analytics and People Analytics and Insights functions, respectively. Michael began his professional career as a client facing consultant for Mercer's Human Capital practice focused on HR Strategy, Organizational Design/ Development and Human Capital Analytics. Michael worked for Mercer in Chicago, Dubai and New York. His master's degree is in Human Resources and Industrial Relations from the University of Illinois and his PhD is in Industrial and Organizational Psychology.

This page is intentionally left blank

Acknowledgement

This book is dedicated to my wife, Christine, who accuses me often of being way "nerdier" now than when she met me. She is right. And she loves me for it. She is my everything and she made this book a reality.

This page is intentionally left blank

Table of Contents

1 Introduction   **13**

1.1 What is "HR Analytics?" 14
1.2 The Art and Science of it All 16
1.3 The Four Roles of HR Analytics 17
Chapter Summary 27
Quiz 1 28
The Rest of this Book 30

2 Recruiting and Staffing   **31**

2.1 Generic Staffing Model 32
2.2 Job Analysis 33
2.3 Sourcing 41
2.4 Recruiting 42
2.5 Reliability 48
2.6 Validity 52
2.7 Words of Caution in Using Assessments 55
2.8 Metrics 59
Chapter Summary 61
Case Study: Physical Therapy Recruiting 62
Quiz 2 69

3 Total Rewards   **75**

3.1 Job Evaluation 76
3.2 Salary Surveys and Benchmarking 79
3.3 Incentives and Pay-for-Performance 84
3.4 Evaluation of Benefits 88
3.5 Metrics 89
Chapter Summary 90
Case Study: Incentive Plan Return On Investment 91
Quiz 3 95

4   Training, Succession and Careers   97

4.1 Competency Modeling   98

4.2 Training Needs Assessment   104

4.3 Training Measurement and Experimental Design   109

4.4 Regression Modeling and Causality   115

4.5 Analytics in Succession and Career Planning   116

4.6 Succession Planning   118

4.7 Metrics   119

Chapter Summary   121

Case Study: ManuCo Succession Planning   122

Quiz 4   132

5   Nonexempt Workforce   135

5.1 Why focus here?   136

5.2 Hourly Hiring   137

5.3 Utility Analysis   138

5.4 Collective Bargaining   139

5.5 Productivity Analysis   146

5.6 Absenteeism   147

5.7 Metrics   148

Chapter Summary   150

Case Study: ManuCo Hourly Hiring Utility Analysis   151

Quiz 5   164

6   Getting Started   167

6.1 Capability / Readiness Matrix   168

6.2 Recruiting   170

6.3 Training impact   174

6.4 Total Rewards - Pay Equity   177

6.5 Employee Turnover   181

6.6 A Note About Inclusion and Diversity Analysis   184

Chapter Summary   186

Case Study: The Four Roles of HR Analytics   187

Quiz 6   191

7 In Closing 197

Number 1: Know Your Data 198
Number 2: Understand What You Can and Cannot Do (Yet!) 198
Number 3: Know Your Organization 199
Number 4: Think Differently 199
Number 5: "People Should Make People Decisions" 200
Some Closing Thoughts - My Hopes and a Thank You 201
Chapter Summary 202

Appendix: Getting Started with Excel – Video Tutorials 203

Basics of Microsoft Excel 203
The Excel Environment 204
Basic Operations 206
Formatting 207
Data Manipulation and Basic Formulas 208
Pivot Tables 209
Charts and Graphs 210
Slicers 210
Putting It All Together 211
Congratulations! 212

References 213

This page is intentionally left blank

Chapter **1**

Introduction

Chapter one opens with a definition of the concept of HR Analytics as a discipline within the human resources function. This chapter also introduces the four roles of HR Analytics and definitions of each. A "quiz" will help the reader to determine his or her place in the analytics spectrum by self-assessing one's own analytical capability and the readiness of one's organization. An outline of the rest of the book closes out the first chapter.

Key learning objectives include understanding of the following:

- Definition of HR analytics

- Importance of HR analytics as it relates to the HR function and overall organizational success

- The "Four Roles" of HR analytics and definitions of each

- Where the reader falls on the "Roles of Analytics" spectrum

1.1 What is "HR Analytics?"

The topic of HR analytics has become increasingly popular over the last ten years. The chart below depicts Google search interest over that time period. Search interest has increased over 1,600%!

Figure 1.1

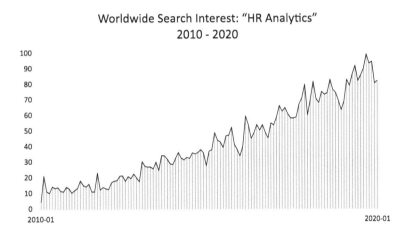

Worldwide Search Interest: "HR Analytics"
2010 - 2020

If we ask 10 people how to define HR analytics, we will probably get 12 different answers. And that's ok. More on that later. For now, let's focus on a broad definition of HR analytics for our purpose as, "the use of data collected on or about people within an organization to make better business decisions."

Given that this definition is so broad, that means that we can use HR Analytics in just about every scenario that could come up, right? Right! This is the power and scope of analytics. We can use data (if we have the right data) to answer just about every question that we might have about an organization, how it works, what motivates employees to exhibit certain behaviors and how to change those behaviors. Once we realize that HR data is all around us and learn how to use it, the sky is truly the limit.

HR Analytics
"The use of data collected on or about people within an organization to make better business decisions."

That means that we can answer questions like, "How can we create a more inclusive culture?" "Inclusive culture" is a pretty nebulous term. A term like that feels kind of "fluffy," but we can quantify that. We can measure that using data.

"What drives retention of our highest performers?" We can measure retention. We can measure performance of our employees and so we can bring those two things together using analytics and measure the factors that lead to greater retention of our highest performing employees.

"What is the best way to predict the performance of our hourly workforce?" So often companies will think of the salaried workforce and how to predict performance of jobs like salespeople or managers. We will learn in a later chapter how the hourly workforce is one of the most untapped sources of data in an organization and how to use those data.

"Why are people really leaving?" Oftentimes our leaders might come to us and say, "Everyone is leaving because of compensation!" or another superlative. Using analytics, we can tease out the real reasons why people are leaving and create recommendations for how to keep those employees who matter most to the organization.

We do all this using a scientific approach. We use this approach to isolate those things that really matter to the question at hand. THAT is the crux of analytics. That is what analytics is all about. It's about teaching us how to ask the right questions, teaching us how to answer those questions and understanding how we can use those data that we have in order to answer those questions.

1.2 The Art and Science of it All

Because numbers are involved, we often think that analytics is all numbers and that there is a right answer. Well, there is a right answer. The trick is that the "right" answer might be different for one organization than another and another. Hopefully, as you read this book, I will demonstrate that, when using data generated by people and about people, analytics becomes part art and part science.

All the preparation that we do before the analysis such as determining the right questions, setting up a field experiment, even structuring the data that we will use in our analysis is a bit of an art form. The decision making that happens prior to the data analysis is just as important and accounts for a lot of the time and effort spent on any given analytics project.

The bottom line is that HR Analytics is absolutely both art and science and not something to be afraid of.

1.3 The Four Roles of HR Analytics

As with many things in life, the roles that one can play in an organization's HR Analytics journey can be summarized into a 2x2 matrix (Figure 1.2). What role can you play? As you will see below, and with any good question, that depends. It depends on the answer to two important questions.

1. Where do you fall on the spectrum of analytical capability?

2. Where does the organization fall in terms of analytical readiness?

When compared to one another, personal capability and organizational readiness create four different roles that an HR practitioner can play. Those roles are Amateur, Advocate, Apprentice, and Advisor.

Each of these roles will be explored in greater detail below.

Figure 1.2   The Four Roles of HR Analytics

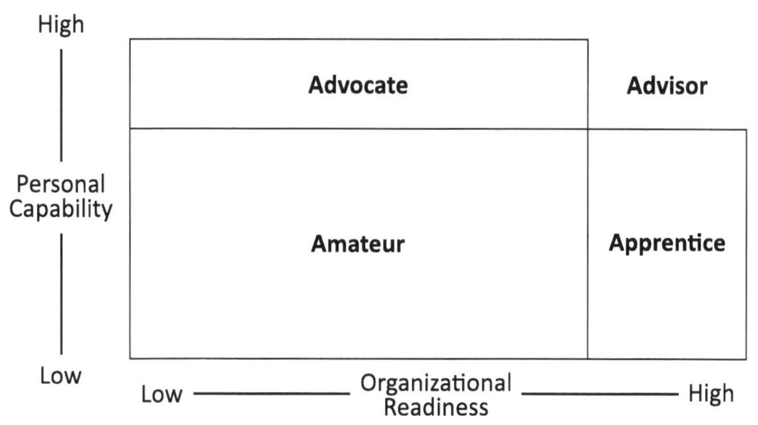

1.3.1 Role 1: Amateur

Amateur. Noun am•a•teur | ˈa-mə-chər: one lacking in experience and competence in an art or science (Merriam-Webster, 2020)

The role of an amateur is defined exactly as listed above. It simply means that you are lacking in the experience and competence in an art or science. In this case, that art *and* science is HR analytics. Professionals who are first starting out in the analytics discipline simply do not have the experience needed to better understand and use analytics. Hopefully, this book will help to change your mind if you fall into that category.

Perhaps the first thing you will notice about the capability and readiness matrix is that the box for amateur is the largest in the matrix. This is intentional. Because it can take a lot of time and effort to advance your skills and influence organizational readiness, this quadrant is the biggest.

If you fall into the amateur quadrant there are several things that you can do in order to increase your personal capability. The first is finishing this book! Second, there are several resources available to anyone online who may want to increase your analytical capability. Some of these resources are focused on technical capability such as how to manipulate data and perform analytics in various software packages. Other resources available will help you to better understand the business issues that organizations face and how to apply analytics to those issues. Another place to go for resources are the "hard" sciences such as chemistry or biology to help you better understand the scientific method and how to conduct field experiments. More on conducting field experiments later in this book.

The other factor that we must consider in the amateur bucket is organizational readiness. This is the hardest factor to change, which is another reason why the amateur quadrant is so large. Changing organizational readiness requires a multi-month or even year-long effort to help the organization better understand how to use analytics. In my experience, this is one of the hardest things that an HR practitioner must endeavor to accomplish. The journey from low readiness to high readiness contains many steps forward and several steps backwards along the way. Because changing organizational readiness is not as easy as going out to a website and learning about technical expertise or statistics, it often takes a very long time.

When starting in the amateur quadrant, in order to move the organizational readiness from low to high the first thing you should do is focus on your own personal capability. Once you have increased your personal capability, bringing the organization along for the journey will be much easier. At that point you will be able to demonstrate value using analytics and help organizational leaders to better understand how analytics can play a role in decision-making.

1.3.2 Role 2: Advocate

Advocate. Noun ad·vo·cate | ˈad-və-kət: one who supports or promotes the interests of a cause or group (Merriam-Webster, 2020)

Once your personal capability has increased to the point of being an advocate, you are now ready to help the organization understand how analytics can play a role in decision-making. If you had taken the journey from amateur to advocate you can take your newly found knowledge to organizational leaders and help them understand the impact that you can have using data and analytics. If joining an organization from the outside already having acquired those skills, the journey might look a bit different.

In order to help the organization understand the skills and capabilities that you bring you will need to demonstrate "quick wins" that are appropriate for the organization. This could include things like using data to tell stories about organizational issues or to explain the answers to questions that organizational leaders might have. When in the advocate quadrant, you will not do yourself any favors by conducting advanced analytics such as predictive algorithms and or predictive modeling. The organization will likely not be able to digest the information nor will they have an appetite for more. The key to being an advocate is that you are able to communicate with the organization using data in a manner that demonstrates the value of analytics while, at the same time, helps to prime the organizational appetite for more analytics. This increase in analytics can be both from a technical perspective such as moving from dashboards to predictive analytics, but also from a quantity perspective in terms of generating demand for analytics work and projects. The role of the advocate is to educate the organization and therefore create more demand for analytics.

1.3.3 Role 3: Apprentice

Apprentice. Noun ap·pren·tice | ə-ˈpren-təs: one who is learning by practical experience under skilled workers a trade, art, or calling (Merriam-Webster, 2020)

The third role that we will talk about is the role of an apprentice. If you fall into this quadrant, your personal capability is low and the organizational readiness is high. This means that people in your organization likely have more skill and experience in analytics than you do. The good news is this is not a bad thing. You can use those people as mentors and teachers as you go on your personal journey to learn more about analytics. In this quadrant, the focus of an HR professional should be to gain experience and skill in order to move to the advisor quadrant.

Internal resources are often a great place to start for learning more about how to use analytics in your organization. Not only do they bring a technical expertise, but they often understand how to apply that expertise to the organization. Because the contextual environment dictates so much about how the organization views analytics and the interpretation of those analytics, having an internal mentor or coach is a great idea for anyone, but especially if you fall into the apprentice quadrant.

While working with an internal mentor or coach, you can also gain technical experience with external resources (such as this book!) or other resources that are widely available. The great part about being an apprentice is that you will be able to immediately apply your skills to organizational issues. As you learn new skills, you'll be able to immediately utilize those in your day-to-day life which makes learning much more enjoyable and useful. The apprentice quadrant can be one of the most robust and richest learning experiences of an HR practitioner's career.

1.3.4 Role 4: Advisor

Advisor. Noun ad·vis·er | əd- 'vī-zər: someone who gives advice (Merriam-Webster, 2020)

You might notice that the advisor quadrant is the smallest quadrant in the matrix. You might also notice that there are no borders on the top or right side of the quadrant. This is very intentional. Because your personal capability will continue to develop and organizational readiness will (hopefully) continue to increase, the goal for the advisor quadrant is to stay in sync with the organization. For example, an individual who falls into high personal capability and whose organization has high organizational readiness for analytics may suggest that an organizational network analysis (Organizational Network Analysis (ONA) is a very advanced type of analysis that can help isolate how information flows within an organization. Because it is necessary to understand who is communicating with one another, the analytics team will collect emails, phone records, chat records, etc. Although the outputs can be very valuable to an organization, you can imagine that not all organizations are ready for this type of analysis) This person may have the capability to conduct the analysis, gather the data, analyze the data, and create recommendations; however if the organization is not ready for that specific type of analysis, there may be further work to be done in change management to ensure that the organization does not reject the analysis. If, for example, business leaders find out that an analytics professional has been collecting emails in order to conduct the organizational network analysis, some might find that a bit concerning. This would require that, before the analysis was done, the rationale, benefits, and value to the organization are explained in detail. In that example, even though that person might be playing the role of an advisor most of the time, for that particular analysis, she may fall back into the advocate quadrant.

Like the amateur quadrant, the advisor quadrant is a sweet spot in the matrix meaning that personal capability aligns to organizational readiness. When an individual is playing the role of advisor, all of the work that goes into collecting the data, running the analysis, managing expectations and gathering feedback, and pulling everything into a succinct story aligns exactly to what the organization is ready to accept. This means that the hard work that the analytics team puts in generates the benefits and outputs from the process that are desired. It is in this quadrant that HR functions can truly demonstrate and harness the power of analytics.

Oftentimes, organizations are not ready for predictive analytics or algorithms until they reach the advisor quadrant. This means that personal capabilities exist to screen and clean the data as well as run the appropriate analysis to conduct the predictive modeling. This also means that the organization has a basic, if not advanced understanding of how predictive analytics work, what they mean, and most importantly, what they don't mean.

As with many 2 x 2 quadrants, you might think that the goal is to eventually reach the upper right right quadrant to become an advisor. That might be true. However, that might not be true. The ultimate goal of the matrix is to help you better understand how you can affect change within the organization using data. The answer to how you can better affect change may differ depending on the group or organization you are working with or for. It may also change based on the leaders within the group or organization.

1.3.5 What are you waiting for? Take the quiz!

Personal Capability

The first part of the equation that we need to explore is your own personal capability. Your capability to conduct and understand analytics is one of the most important aspects of figuring out what role you can play in your organization's analytics journey. The good news is that your capability is fluid. It can change. If you want or need to further develop your analytical capability, there are many resources available (including this book!). The key to your personal role in analytics is to figure out how your personal capability relates to your organization's readiness.

Organizational Readiness

Would you give a new driver a Ferrari to drive? No way! Neither would I.

Would you give a new driver an SUV to drive? Maybe? Yeah, that seems about right.

Would you give a new driver an old four door sedan to drive? For sure! Me too.

The point of this is that organizations, like newly minted drivers need time behind the wheel, need time and experience with HR Analytics before they can be used appropriately. In the discipline of HR Analytics, many practitioners strive to reach for "predictive" analytics out of the gate. This is the pinnacle of analytics and algorithms. Can we predict performance? Can we predict who is going to stay or leave? These are great questions to endeavor to answer if the organization is ready for them. In my experience, organizations are not ready for predictive analytics and structural equation modeling. Many organizations are barely ready for correlations. This makes the task of organizational assessment so critical.

In order to figure out which of the four roles of HR Analytics you can play, answer the questions listed below from 1 – 5 (1 = Strongly Disagree; 5 = Strongly Agree). After you have rated each statement, calculate a total for questions 1 – 5 (Personal Capability) and a total for questions 6 – 10 (Organizational Readiness). Use those totals to plot where you fall on the Capability / Readiness Matrix and determine the role that you could play.

Personal Ability	I am comfortable conducting applied research in an organizational setting.	
	I know how to apply statistics to solve an organizational need.	
	I can manipulate data in a spreadsheet or data analysis tool (eg MS Excel, Google Sheets,SPSS, etc.)	
	I am comfortable using data to communicate my ideas.	
	I can condense a large amount of qualitative data (e.g., interview notes) into meaningful trends or themes.	
	Personal Ability Total	
Organizational Readiness	My organization uses data to make decisions on a regular basis.	
	Leaders within my organization are comfortable interpreting data from charts.	
	My organization has a formal "business analytics" function.	
	My organization looks to improve the way things are done.	
	My organization has formal training for employees to learn about analytics.	
	Organizational Readiness Total	
Your Role:		

Your Role In Analytics

Your role = Personal capability x Organizational readiness

Figure 1.3

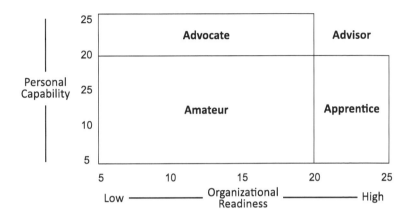

Just like analytics as a discipline, the matrix above is a bit of art and a bit of science. It is worth noting that your position in the matrix can change. It can change over time as you become more capable. It can change as your organization changes. It can change from group to group within an organization. The intention is to give you a sense of where to start when addressing the analytical needs of an organization, based upon the skills that you bring to the table.

You might notice that, to become an "Advisor" or "Apprentice" is a bit harder (i.e., the boxes are smaller). That is intentional. This is because, often, to move an organization from low readiness to high readiness is much harder than to change your own personal capabilities. Often, changing organizational readiness for analytics requires a culture change which can take months, if not years. Do not let that discourage you. Each step on the journey of organizational readiness is part of preparing the organization for advanced analytics in the future. Each step is a necessary stop along the way and leaders within your organization will thank you for helping to bring the organization into a place where decisions can be more thoughtfully made using data and analytics.

Chapter Summary

◆ HR Analytics is the use of data collected on or about people within an organization to make better business decisions.

◆ HR Analytics is a combination of both art and science.

◆ Your current role in analytics can be determined by assessing your individual capability and the organizational readiness.

◆ There are four roles of HR analytics – Amateur, Advocate, Apprentice and Advisor.

Quiz 1

1. **What is HR analytics?**

   a. The use of data collected on or about people within an organization to make better business decisions

   b. Something that is too "fuzzy" to define

   c. The study of how human resources functions are organized

   d. The study of the history of human resources

2. **Analytics is_____**

   a. All science

   b. Mostly art

   c. A balance of art and science

   d. The greatest thing since sliced bread

3. **Your role in analytics can be determined by assessing what?**

   a. Organizational capability x personal readiness

   b. Personal capability x organizational readiness

   c. Personal capability alone

   d. Organizational readiness alone

4. **In the roles matrix, the box for amateur is the biggest. Why?**

   a. It was a typo

   b. It takes a long time and a lot of effort to develop your personal skills and prepare the organization for deeper analytics

   c. Because more people will fall into the category

   d. Because it is geometrically pleasing

5. **When first starting out in HR analytics, you should what?**

   a. Go as fast as you can – the clock is ticking

   b. Make sure you burn a few bridges along the way

   c. Give up. It's not worth the effort

   d. Take your time to build your own skills while building up organizational capability – walk before you run

*Solutions to the above questions can be downloaded from the **Online Resources** section of this book on* **www.vibrantpublishers.com**

The Rest of this Book

This book is meant to be a practical guide to help you better understand how to apply analytics to your day to day life as an HR practitioner. We will walk through many ways in which we can use data and analytics to answer some of the biggest questions that an organization might have about its workforce. The book is structured around several (not all) functional disciplines within the HR function. At the end of each chapter, there is a case study to help you practice the key lessons. Companion videos help to drive home the main points and provide technical guidance on how to perform many of the analyses in Microsoft Excel. I sincerely hope that you enjoy this book and I hope that it helps you along your journey of HR Analytics.

Chapter **2**

Recruiting and Staffing

$\mathcal{S}$taffing and Recruiting is one of the HR functions where gut instinct and intuition is most often used. Within the realm of staffing, analytics can help us to find better candidates in a shorter period, maybe. We need to make sure that we are using analytical techniques properly. This chapter will describe some ways that we can use analytics and some of the cautionary tales of doing so. Analytics can be such a powerful tool in the staffing process; however, many organizations do not understand the proper way to utilize them.

Key learning objectives for this chapter include knowledge of the following topics:

- A generic staffing model and process

- How analytics can apply to the various stages of the staffing process

- How we can use analytics to inform the job analysis process

- How to code qualitative data and what to do with it once it is coded

- When to use and when not to use hiring assessments for the salaried workforce

- Reliability and validity concepts and why they are important

- Various staffing metrics

- Applying the knowledge gained by completing the case study at the end of the chapter

It should be stated that this book is not intended to be an exhaustive reference for the staffing process. Should you want to learn about staffing in depth, there are many resources available via a simple internet or library search. We will, however, discuss a generic staffing model and some of the places in that model where analytics can help us to make better and faster decisions.

2.1 Generic Staffing Model

When we think about the staffing model, it is helpful to think about it as a funnel with a filter attached. In this analogy, things go into the funnel, some things are filtered out, and the rest go through to the end. In other words, a lot of things go into the process, and many fewer come out on the other side. Using analytics, we can make sure the things that come out the other side are the right things, and that they go through those filters in an expedient manner.

2.2 Job Analysis

Before we even get to the first step in our staffing model funnel, we first need to understand the job itself. One way we can do that is through a job analysis. At its root, job analysis is the process through which we study and describe requirements and rewards for a given position (Heneman, Judge, & Kammeyer-Mueller, 2003). The first step of the job analysis is to identify specific tasks and the context for a particular job (Gael, 1988). In order to achieve this, there are several ways to conduct the job analysis. Some of those ways include direct observation, historical research, questionnaires, and interviews (Heneman, Judge, & Kammeyer-Mueller, 2003). Direct observation entails watching someone perform the job and taking notes about the tasks and requirements that are necessary to complete the job successfully. Historical research includes academic and industrial focused research about the job. Job task questionnaires could also be sent to job incumbents or people who have had that job in the past. Finally, interviews can be done with incumbents, supervisors, and peers in order to better understand the requirements of the job. Although each method has its own pros and cons, we are going to focus on the use of interviews for the purposes of this text.

Job analysis can also take on several different types, such as competency-based, job requirements-based, or rewards-based. For our purposes, we will focus on job requirements-based interviews (see Table 2.1 below). Keep in mind that this section is not about interviewing internal or external candidates for the job. We are focused on interviews of incumbents and their supervisors, in order to fully understand the requirements of the job. This section will help to demonstrate how qualitative data analysis can apply to job analysis and further understanding of a position. Although qualitative data analysis techniques can be applied to many other disciplines, conducting interviews for a job analysis can generate a significant amount of qualitative data, and is a good example of when to use these techniques. In this case, we are using job analysis as an example of primary qualitative research, along with the methods to boil down those myriad data points into meaningful categories.

Table 2.1   **Methods of Job Analysis**

		Type of Job Analysis		
		Competency	Rewards	Job Requirements (KSAO)
Data Gathering Method	Existing Information			
	Observation			
	Interviews			Our current focus
	Questionnaires			

Primary Data Collection through Interviews

Conducting interviews is one method of primary data collection. Primary data collection is the process through which we collect data from original sources (Sekaran & Bougie, 2016). This contrasts with *secondary data collection*, which we might do for a research study based on existing literature.

An interview is a guided and purposeful conversation between two or more people. There are two types of interviews we will discuss. The first is an *unstructured interview*. This is where the interviewer will go into a conversation without a planned sequence of questions. The interviewer will "go with the flow" and see where the conversations go.

The second type of interview is a *structured interview*. These are conducted when it is known at the outset what information you need to gather from the participant, and you have a predetermined set of questions you will be asking. No one way is better than another, and oftentimes, researchers will use a combination of both structured and unstructured interviews. That way, if you deviate or go off course during the interview, you can always come back to the structured questions.

Pros and Cons of a Personal Interview

One very common method of conducting an interview is called a *personal interview*. This is what we typically think about when interviewing another person. The interviewer sits down face-to-face (in person or virtually) with the other person, to conduct an interview just like they do on the news.

Advantages

- The participant can clarify any doubts or questions about the questionnaire.

- The interviewer can pick up on nonverbal cues.

- There are relatively high response rates and cooperation.

- We can use special visual aids and scoring devices during the interview.

Disadvantages

- In-person interviews can cost a lot of money and are time intensive.

- Potential geographical limitations exist. Sometimes someone will have to fly in for an interview, or drive a great distance for an interview, which can be costly, although video conferencing makes this less and less of an issue.

- Confidentiality concerns can also be an issue with face-to-face interviews.

- Some respondents might be unwilling to talk to strangers.

- Interview training can be time intensive and require skills practice and training to master.

Coding and Categorizing Our Qualitative Data

The definition of *qualitative data* is simply "the data in the form of words." Examples might be interview notes, the transcripts of focus groups, answers to open-ended questions we might send out in a survey, transcription of video recordings, accounts of experience with a product on the Internet, and news articles.

When we analyze qualitative data, we are trying to boil down these data to make valid inferences about the topic at hand. Think about, for example, the number of notes you might have based on an interview or the transcript of a TV show. These are large quantities of data that we are trying to reduce into something that we can analyze. We then need to display those data so we can draw conclusions and verify that those conclusions are true. We will walk through those steps below.

The first step in data reduction is *coding*. Coding is the analytic process through which the qualitative data is reduced, rearranged, and integrated to form a theory (Serkan and Bougie, 2016). Basically, we are giving each of our notes a label. The process of labelling notes can be very iterative, based on the other data that we have collected, and labels should be revisited throughout the interview analysis process.

It is important to decide what level of coding we will use. For example, will we code our interview statements by paragraph? By sentence? By word? Each of these are possibilities and it is ultimately up to the researcher to decide which level of analysis to use.

Next, we need to categorize those codes by arranging and organizing them into various groups. This is a process we undergo as we are thinking through these data, and the number of categories could be as many as we need. For example, we may interview one person and code the notes into four categories. However, based on the next interview, we may discover a fifth category that was not mentioned in the first interview. So, then we would return to our first set of four-category notes and recategorize them into the five categories, which could potentially change the code for certain notes. Depending on the number of interviews we conduct, we may want to repeat this process several times. This allows for flexibility in our sorting, and creativity in our analysis.

Sample Coding of Interview Notes

The statements below from a job analysis interview could be coded into themes that help reduce the data into manageable "buckets" of information.

"Well, I would say that the person in this job needs to be able to talk to others in a nice way, you know, make friends with people. Show that they care. There is also an aspect of the job where the person needs to be creative when they talk to our customers. Our customers call with some pretty crazy requests!"

We could potentially code the example above into several competencies like: "customer focus innovation, team orientation, adaptability," etc. It is up to the researcher(s) to not only decide on the level of analysis, but also determine the correct coding for the information. This is another example of art and science in HR analytics.

Refer to the video **Qualitative Data Coding.mp4** in **Online Resources** section of this book on **www.vibrantpublishers.com**

Once we have our categories determined, we need to figure out the best way to display the data. The display we choose depends on the story we are trying to tell. One helpful way to show qualitative data is a word cloud.

Figure 2.1

Word clouds are available on several programs, including Microsoft PowerPoint and Word. The size of the word is directly related to the number of times that word is mentioned in the text. Word clouds are popular for briefly displaying what might be important in a group of texts.

A Few Quick Notes on Reliability and Validity of Qualitative Research

There are two main things that we need to pay attention to when it comes to qualitative research. They are *reliability* and *validity*. (There are many great resources which go into much more detail about these concepts. This section is simply meant to be a primer and acknowledgement of these concepts.)

Reliability

Within qualitative research, reliability has two different types. The first is *category reliability*, which depends on the analyst's ability to formulate categories and present definitions of the categories to competent judges so they will agree on which items of a certain population belong in a category, and which do not. (Kassarjian, 1977). In other words, this type of reliability answers the question, "Do the categories the researcher came up with make sense to experts?"

The second type of reliability is *inter-judge reliability*. Inter-judge reliability can be defined as the degree of consistency between coders processing the same data (Kassarjian, 1977). This type of reliability answers the question, "If you give one person the data set and another person the same data set, would they be consistent in how they coded the data?"

Validity

The last piece that should be mentioned when it comes to qualitative research is *validity*. There are two types of validity in qualitative research.

The first type of validity is *internal validity*. The question we are trying to answer is, "Do these categories accurately represent the collected data?"

The second type of validity is *external validity* which answers the question, "Can we generalize...or settings?" The answer is, "Sometimes." Cultural nuances and various ways of working can prevent broad generalizations from one organization to the next. This makes the findings from one organization to another difficult to compare.

2.3 Sourcing

The first bucket in our funnel is sourcing our candidates. *Sourcing candidates* simply means finding candidates for the position for which we are hiring (Heneman, et al., 2003). There are many different places where we can find candidates; the hard part is to determine which of those places give us the best candidates. There really is no "best" place to find candidates though, and it really depends on what you're looking for in the position. Several criteria can be used to determine sourcing options for candidates, such as the quantity of labor, the quality of labor, the availability of that source, past experiences, budget, and contractual obligations (Heneman, et al., 2003). Analytics can help us to understand several of those criteria, and the output of various sources, for tapping-into.

Pro Tip

When determining a sourcing strategy, make sure that the organization is using empirical data to select and maintain relationships with various recruiting sources. Oftentimes, those relationships are built simply on personal basis and are not reviewed with a critical lens.

When it comes to sourcing candidates for a job, organizations often rely on current employees and their networks. Take for example, the recruitment from graduate programs in human resources. Oftentimes, the organization will either have experience from a graduate program, or senior executives within the organization may have graduated from a particular program.

Usually those programs rise to the top of the list when determining places to return for recruitment. What those organizations do not typically do well is quantifying the cost and benefit of using those sources to find candidates.

2.4 Recruiting

Analytics in the recruiting step of the staffing model can also be helpful but are often overlooked by organizations trying to hire as quickly as possible. To define *recruiting*, we will think about the steps that immediately follow the sourcing process. That means we have already determined where we are going to find our candidates and are now trying to communicate with them about the organization, its values, and the job opportunity that is available.

Analytics can help us in this phase of the process primarily with the messages and vehicles through which we are sending those messages, to potential candidates. For example, a startup technology firm who is trying to convey the message of being fast, nimble, and technologically advanced, would likely not want to advertise in a traditional "help-wanted" section of the newspaper. Instead, they may rely on personal relationships, LinkedIn, or other means of electronic communication. On the other hand, a manufacturing organization who is starting a greenfield site in a town of less than a thousand people, might use printed flyers in the local grocery stores, or even different means of communicating with potential candidates.

Analytics can help us to determine the right method by which we communicate with candidates. It also helps us determine the right messages needed to attract the right candidates for the job.

2.4.1 Screening / Selection Using Assessments

This section will dive deeper into the uses for HR analytics in the realm of hiring assessments. You will learn about why assessments are important, the definition and rationale for using constructs, the importance of reliability and validity, and some additional words of caution that all HR professionals can use when it comes to evaluating hiring assessments.

First and foremost, let's define a *hiring assessment*. An assessment is simply another name for a test that measures something that a company or organization would find useful in the workplace. Assessments are used for all sorts of reasons. One reason that an organization might use an assessment is to speed up their hiring process. For example, if you need to hire hundreds or thousands of employees at once, you may want to use an assessment to filter out those people who would not be a good fit for the characteristics of the job. Companies could also use assessments because they might be (in some instances) more accurate than individual judgments of candidates. Another reason to use assessments is that some organizations want to measure things that are simply not observable, such as integrity.

2.4.2 What do Assessments Measure?

At the end of the day, assessments are used to measure things, like skills that would be useful on the job, personality traits, attitudes, and values that align to organizational goals. Ultimately, we use assessments to attempt to measure a person's future performance on the job and help to sort candidates into categories based on this prediction of performance. The type and number of categories the candidates are divided into are dependent on the organization and how the assessments are being used. For example, an organization might want to test candidates on the ability to lift a heavy object. That organization could conduct a simple assessment where candidates are required to lift a 25-pound weight. The assessment results would then group candidates into categories of those who can lift the weight, and those who cannot. Based on those categories, those who could not lift the weight would be screened out of the process, saving the time and money it would require by putting those candidates through the rest of the process.

Rationale for Using an Assessment
- Efficiency
- Accuracy (maybe)
- Ability to measure unobservable traits

2.4.3 Constructs: What are They and Why do we use Them?

One term that gets thrown around a lot when people talk about assessments is the notion of a *construct*. In order to clear up some of the confusion, let's talk for a few minutes about what a construct is and why we use it.

A construct is simply a category that is measured using an assessment. Because constructs cannot be observed like a behavior, we need to use a proxy or proxies to measure these constructs. For example, we can't easily measure something like integrity, so an organization might deploy an assessment to measure the construct of integrity. We measure constructs in order to group people based on their scores for these various constructs. The goal or the intention is that these groups will hopefully perform differently in the workplace, and we can use these groups to effectively filter out good and bad candidates for our jobs.

2.4.4 Assessments Dissected

Assessments generally consist of two parts. The first part is a *predictor or predictors*. The predictor is the construct that the assessment is designed to measure such as integrity, for example. In other words, the predictor is the independent variable we use to attempt to guess the result of the dependent variable or criterion.

Construct
A category that is measured using an assessment.

The second part is the criteria or criterion, are those outcomes on the job for which the assessment was designed. For example, if we have an assessment that uses a construct of integrity, the criterion might be that we are looking for people who will not steal things from the workplace.

When you are designing or evaluating an assessment, it is critical that you make sure your predictors in your criterion are related. It is generally a good idea to start with academic research about the criterion that you are trying to measure. Academic research tends to be less biased than industry research, and it is put through a rigorous peer review process. Once you have investigated the academic research, it is time you use some analytical skills of your own to better understand what you are measuring and how it is related to the desired behaviors on the job. We're going to talk about a few ways that we can do that in this section.

The most important thing we should remember about hiring assessments is that we are purposeful about how and when we use them. Oftentimes, organizations will implement a hiring assessment without doing the due diligence or research about how it was designed or intended to be used. Although this might allow the organization to implement the assessment in a more timely fashion, a lack of understanding about the assessment could result in either hiring lots of bad candidates, or missing out on good candidates, not to mention the time and money that would be wasted.

2.4.5 Reliability and Validity

Pro Tip

Another thing that we need to balance is fairness and bias in the hiring process. Because this is not an unemployment law book, we will not go into all the legal ramifications of assessments. However, you should work with your legal counsel to ensure that your overall process and each individual piece of the process does not discriminate against a particular group. More information on discrimination in hiring can be found at governmental websites.

These terms are used frequently by a lot of people when talking about assessments, though, not everyone knows what they mean and what their implications are. While I don't expect that every HR practitioner is able to fully calculate reliability and validity, it is necessary to understand the concepts and why they are important. *Reliability and validity* are not just for assessment designers but are just as important to those who are using or implementing those assessments in the workplace. They help you to understand how the assessments are related to the job for which you are hiring, and how accurate they are at predicting actual job performance.

2.4.6 The Silver Bullet?

It is important to remember that no test is perfect in design or execution, and because we use statistics to validate and create assessments, there will always be instances when we have error. For example, there will always be someone you hire because he or she did a great job on the assessment and who, after being on the job for several months, demonstrates that he or she is not a good fit for the job. In "assessment speak" we call that a *false positive*. You might also choose to pass by a candidate who did poorly on the assessment, but who would have been a great hire. We call that a *false negative*. The idea in using HR analytics related to assessments is to use our knowledge of analytics, statistics, and assessment methodologies (reliability and validity) to minimize the number of false positives and false negatives in the hiring process. If you have an assessment that is designed for the job AND is valid and reliable, that is the best you can do.

Because no test is perfect, we must use assessments as just one data point in the hiring process, not the whole process. Assessments should be used as part of the hiring process, in combination with several other data points about each candidate, in order to make hiring decisions. When using an off-the-shelf assessment (one that you did not design yourself), it is critical that you review the assessment manual to ensure the test was designed for the intended audience and the job for which is being used.

For example, if we are hiring for an administrative assistant position, it would likely be inappropriate to use an assessment that was designed to select iron workers. Assessing the appropriateness of using a assessment is why we need to understand reliability and validity.

2.5 Reliability

First, I want to define *reliability*. Reliability answers the question of, "How well does the test measure the same thing over and over again?" In other words, if we take it now and we take the same test in a year, will I get a similar result? Reliability is important because if we do not have a reliable test, we cannot be assured that the results we are seeing could be replicated.

To measure reliability, we use something called a reliability coefficient. The reliability coefficient is denoted by the letter R and is a simple correlation from 0 to 1. Having a reliability coefficient of zero (0) means that the test is not reliable at all and having a reliability coefficient of one (1), means that the assessment is perfectly reliable. In the real world, however, we never actually see a one (1) when it comes to reliability. In the table below, you can view the U.S. Department of Labor guidelines for how to interpret various reliability coefficients. These are still the gold standard when it comes to interpreting these coefficients (mostly because they are defensible in a court of law).

Table 2.2 General Guidelines for Interpreting Reliability Coefficients

Reliability Coefficient Value	Interpretation
.90 and up	Excellent
.80 – .89	Good
.70 – .79	Adequate
Below .70	May have limited applicability

Saad, S., Carter, G. W., Rothenberg, M., & Israelson, E. (1999). Testing and Assessment: An Employer's Guide to Good Practices.

A word of caution - we should not reject an assessment just because it has a low reliability. The overall context of the situation and type of test must also be considered. When trying to measure the effectiveness of an assessment, it is essential that we use our critical thinking skills and gather as much data as we can about the assessments being used. We cannot make decisions based solely on one measurement or another.

There are several types of reliability estimates. The first type of reliability estimate is the *test- retest estimate*. This measures the correlation between my score if I take the test now (Score 1) and then take it later (Score 2). To calculate the test-retest estimate, we calculate a Pearson Correlation Coefficient between my first result and my second result and see if they are correlated (this is a basic correlation that can be done in Excel).

The next type of reliability is called a *parallel-form* reliability. This measures the scores, or the similarity of the scores, between one form of the assessment and another. For example, if we wanted to measure the reliability of a numerical reasoning test, we would split the questions into two groups (Test A and Test B). We would then administer Test A to a group of individuals on Friday, and Test B to those same individuals a week later. After collecting the results from each test, we would correlate the results to see if they are related.

The third type of reliability is an *inter-rater* reliability. In order to calculate this type of reliability, we would have the same test scored by two qualified individuals. We would then calculate the correlation between the scores from each of those individuals. For example, if I am an Olympic diver (that, I am not!) and I then perform a dive, would the final scores of the judges correlate, and/ if so, to what extent? We use the Pearson Correlation Coefficient to determine the degree of relatedness.

The final type of reliability that we will discuss in this section is called *internal-consistency* reliability, and it is measured by calculating a statistic called Chronbach's alpha. This statistic measures the strength of the groupings of items into their underlying constructs. In an assessment, there will likely be several different items that measure one construct. For example, several questions would measure something like integrity. Internal-consistency reliability measures the connection between those items. In other words, when compared to other items on the assessment, do the items that we think measure integrity "hang together?"

 Refer to the video **Chronbach's Alpha.mp4** in **Online Resources** section of this book on **www.vibrantpublishers.com**

2.5.1 Standard Error of Measurement

Assessment designers will often provide another important statistic that is related to reliability. This measure is called the *standard error of measurement*. Although it is a fancy name, we refer to this in our everyday vernacular when we say that a result is, "X, plus or minus some percentage." For example, during elections when news outlets report that a particular candidate received X percent of the vote plus or minus 5 percent," they are reporting on the standard error of measurement. In this case, there is a recognition that the survey methodology is not perfect and contains some amount of error. This statistic is used because reliability measures, as we talked about earlier, are not perfect.

When using the standard error of measurement in assessments, using that same logic of the fallibility of assessments recognizes that any given participant's "real" score falls somewhere within the standard error of measurement. For example, if someone scores a 100 on an assessment with the standard error of two, that candidate's true score would be somewhere between 98 and 102. The important thing to remember is that the smaller the standard error, the more accurate the assessment, or the smaller the window of error. Another important note in our journey to find the right assessment is that even if the test is reliable, and has a small standard of error, it still might not be valid. It is often said, "reliability is necessary, but not sufficient." This leads us to our next topic of validity.

 Refer to the video **Standard Error of Measurement.mp4** in **Online Resources** section of this book on **www.vibrantpublishers.com**

2.6 Validity

The most important measure to observe when evaluating the usability of an assessment is *validity*. Validity measures how well the assessment measures what it is supposed to measure. It tells you how well the test results relate to behaviors on the job for which the assessment was designed. Validity gives context and meaning to the assessment scores.

Validity is important because what is valid for one job might not be valid for another. For example, a test that is considered valid for a mechanic job may not be valid for an office job, and vice versa. There will be more about the pitfalls of off-the-shelf assessments later in this section, but it is up to you and your judgment to determine if the assessment chosen is sufficiently valid for your intentions.

Bottom Line
Validity tells you if a test is useful or not.

There are several ways to measure validity that fall into one of two groups, *content-related* or *criterion-related*. Content-related validity measures the appropriateness of the content of the assessment. In other words, does the content of the assessment "make sense" for what it is trying to measure? Criterion-related validity measure the extent to which the assessment results are related to other measures, such as job performance. Criterion-related validity is more time intensive and harder to obtain; however, the more time and effort that goes into collecting these data, the more confidence we can have in the usefulness of our assessment.

Making a judgement about validity is part science and part art. Because we are using statistics for validation, we know that there will be some error; however, it is incumbent on us, as the evaluator of the assessment, to gather a body of evidence about the appropriateness of the assessment. Each of the methods below are legitimate ways to validate an assessment; however, some mean more than others.

2.6.1 Content-Related Validity

The first (and most basic) form of validity is called *face validity*. This measures the extent to which the assessment appears to measure what it claims to measure. Often, assessment designers will ask people who have taken the test, or who have an interest in the assessment, to rate the questions (not necessarily subject matter experts). Face validity is considered "robust" only when a "reasonable" level of agreement exists between raters (lots of art, and a little less science in face validity). It should also be noted, that just because an assessment has face validity, does not mean that it actually measures what it purports to measure, only that the raters think it does.

The second type of content-related validity is called *construct validity*. This type of validation answers the question of, "Does the test measure what it claims to measure?" More complicated than face validity, construct- related validity measures the interpretations of the scores on the assessment related to theoretical terms. For example, a measure of integrity must be related to the theoretical model of integrity. Construct-related validation is often used for abstract traits, like numerical reasoning or learning agility. This is usually performed using advanced statistical models, such as factor modelling, which is not covered in this section.

2.6.2 Criterion-Related Validity

The first type of criterion-related validity is called *concurrent validity*. An assessment is said to have concurrent validity when the current test is sufficiently related to an existing test of the same or similar content. What is sufficient? That depends. It depends on the type of assessment, the circumstances under which the assessment is being used, the existing assessment to which it is being compared, and on and on. Again, a great example of when analytics can be a combination of art and science.

At the top of the validation hierarchy is *predictive validation*. Predictive validation measures the statistical relationship between individual assessment results and some event or other criterion that occurs in the future, such as actual performance on the job. This means that an organization would need to collect test scores throughout the hiring process, hire those candidates based on some other measure (such as interviews), observe those same people on the job, and then calculate the relationship between their original test score with how they perform on the job (specific measures could be individual performance, safety, absenteeism, sales, etc.). This is the gold standard when it comes to validity measurement, though it can be very time-consuming and expensive to calculate.

Just like reliability, there are certain guidelines that should be considered for assessing the validity of an assessment. You can see those guidelines in the table below. Criterion validity is a correlation between results on the test and performance on the job. Similar to reliability values, the scores can be between zero and one, though they hardly ever exceed .40 in the real world.

Table 2.3   General Guidelines for Interpreting Validity Coefficients

Reliability Coefficient Value	Interpretation
Above .35	Very beneficial
.21 – .35	Likely to be useful
.11 – .20	Depends on circumstances
Below .11	Unlikely to be useful

Saad, S., Carter, G. W., Rothenberg, M., & Israelson, E. (1999). Testing and Assessment: An Employer's Guide to Good Practices.

It is important to remember that conducting a validation study in your organization can take time and cost a lot of money, so organizations often rely on external parties for assessments. A few words of caution are below.

2.7 Words of Caution in Using Assessments

This section has highlighted several different areas of assessments, and how HR analytics can help to calculate the utility of an assessment. It is critically important that you understand how assessments can be used and how they can be measured in terms of their appropriateness for the job at hand. Some further words of caution when using assessments are below.

2.7.1 Beware of "Best Practice"

Oftentimes, external vendors will offer solutions that are directly off-the-shelf and will claim to hire "quality" candidates based on best practice. When it comes to assessments and the constructs that are being measured, we really need to consider organizational context. That means that there are no "best practices." We need to understand the organization, the values of the organization, the things that are important to the job, and how those things are demonstrated in everyday work behaviors. For example, a plant manager in one organization might have very different job responsibilities and skills needed, than a plant manager in another organization. If you were to use an assessment based on a general plant manager description, you may have many false positives or false negatives in the hiring process.

2.7.2 Understand Your Population

When evaluating an assessment, we must make sure that we understand the population on which the validation studies were done. Often, validation studies provided by external vendors will be lengthy in words and will describe (in great detail) the studies used to validate an assessment; however, the sample population may not be appropriate for the actual population with which you intend to use the assessment. For example, psychology undergrads are not a great representation of the population at large, nor are they a great representation of any given job, yet many assessments have been validated using psychology undergraduates.

2.7.3 Understand the Tradeoff between Efficiency and Effectiveness

When considering an assessment, it is critically important to consider the cost of a wrong hire. As mentioned before, because we are using statistics and because statistics are not perfect, there will be error in assessments. It is important for the organization to consider the cost of a wrong hire and the cost of missing out on the right hire. For example, if you're hiring an executive who is going to turn around a struggling organization, what are the costs of not getting that perfect hire in that job? Are those costs more, or less, than conducting a thorough assessment? Are there assessments that can isolate those things that are important to that position? Should you create your own assessment based on what's important to the organization? All these things must be considered when implementing or assessing an assessment.

2.7.4 There Will Likely be Adverse Impact

Another note of caution to absolutely consider is the adverse impact of the assessment. Often when using assessments, we will observe some sort of adverse impact. The key is for HR managers to understand the extent of the adverse impact, and how to balance that with other things, like efficiency and errors in the process. Our friends in employment law can help to give guidelines on an appropriate level of adverse impact, should it arise. Giving guidance in a forum such as this would not do justice to the topic and, organizational tolerance differs greatly; therefore, we will not go into greater detail here.

2.7.5 Artificial Intelligence

Currently, there is a push to let analytics do a lot of the work in the recruiting and staffing realm. Many companies are keen to better understand which candidates will perform best on the job and are doing so through assessments and other analytics techniques. Some companies are even going as far as using artificial intelligence to conduct interviews and screen out candidates, based on things like tone-of-voice and facial expressions. Although it would be inappropriate to comment on the appropriateness of such methods, a word of caution would be beneficial.

Understanding statistics and how statistics work is key to understanding how some of these formulas predict future performance. For example, if I measure 500 things throughout the interview process and put them into a regression model, based on performance of employees currently in the job, I can tell you with 100% certainty that a few of those variables would be statistically significant predictors of good performance on the job. Are they good performers on the job? Maybe. However, it could be that those variables are statistically significant simply due to chance alone. There have been several articles written on the "capitalization on chance" in statistics and methodological concerns with using artificial intelligence in the hiring process. Should you have further interest in the topic, I suggest reading some of those articles.

2.7.6 Inherent Bias in Statistical Models

As with any model that is built on historical data, including when we build predictive models, we are naturally building the historical biases of the organization's decisions into those models. For example, if we are trying to predict performance on the job based on a hiring assessment, the outcome variable of performance on the job would have been influenced by the inherent biases of the organization, the managers, and how performance is measured, in order to get us values for that variable. Those biases would then be enforced in the predictive model that is being used. Therefore, it is critically important to understand the organization, the values of the organization, and other working norms before constructing a predictive model. It also highlights the need for objective, not subjective measures of performance when designing a predictive model. With these cautions in mind you should be able to mitigate most issues and proceed accordingly.

Discussion Question:

Given all the pros and cons of using assessments in the staffing and recruiting process, do you think your organization should use them? If so, how? If not, why not?

Solution to the above question can be downloaded from the **Online Resources** section of this book on **www.vibrantpublishers.com**

2.8 Metrics

With all these analyses, is important to understand how to measure and track progress within the staffing and recruiting function. In order to do that, many organizations turn to metrics. The possibilities are endless when it comes to metrics for the staffing process. Because there are so many components of the process, and if we have reliable data, each of those components can be measured and tracked. Some sample metrics are shown below:

- New employee job performance

- New employee turnover

- New hire failure rate

- Manager satisfaction with new hires

- New employee training success

- Cost per hire

- Time to hire

Each of these clearly have pros and cons, and it is important that we understand the culture of the organization and the data that are available in order to use these common metrics. It should also be noted that each of these metrics can be defined differently depending on the organization.

Chapter Summary

◆ The recruiting and staffing function within an organization is one of the most important and process driven function within an organization, making it ripe for HR analytics work.

◆ A generic staffing model can be thought of as a funnel with a filter attached. Lots goes in, but not much comes out the other end of the process.

◆ Job analysis is an important aspect of the recruiting process and sets the foundation for the recruiting strategy and sourcing options.

◆ Qualitative data is very important to collect and can be coded and quantified for useful analysis.

◆ Hiring assessments attempt to measure one's ability to succeed in a job.

◆ Reliability and validity are critical components to understand in an assessment.

CASE STUDY:
Physical Therapy Recruiting

Overview

The following case provides an overview of Steve, the owner and founder of Universal Physical Therapy. Although Steve has a booming business, he is in need of another physical therapist. Not just any physical therapist, but one that fits his company culture. Based on the reading, you will be asked to answer several questions related to the previous chapter.

Introduction

By all accounts, the party was a huge success. The decorations were perfect, the food from a local restaurant down the street was top-notch, and of course, the conversations were lively. As Steve looked around his physical therapy office at his 40th anniversary party, he was extremely proud of the impact that he and his colleagues have had on the community over the years. Throughout those four decades, he treated thousands of patients in the local community, as well as from afar, since his practice was known as the place to go for great care and excellent patient outcomes.

Universal Physical Therapy

In the fall of 1979, Steve Trublowski was a freshly minted physical therapist. He had just graduated from Wayne University with his Master's degree in physical therapy. After completing his residency in the hospitals, Steve took a giant leap of faith in attempting to be the very first (successful) private physical therapy practice in the state of Michigan. So, Steven left the hospital setting and started a new physical therapy practice, located in St. Clair Shores, Michigan. He had relationships with some of the doctors in the area due to his background and education. However, because patients need a physician's referral to see a physical therapist, it was important that Steve develop relationships with even more doctors in the area. Because relationships were so important to the referral rate of any doctor, he also had to make sure that his staff was able to cultivate and create relationships, as well.

For the last 50 years, Steve worked to develop relationships and make an impact within the local community. His number-one priority was excellent patient care, and he treated all his patients like his own family. It is for this reason he was able to grow the business, employing just over 25 employees, including physical therapists, physical therapy assistants, and front office staff.

Company Culture

Universal Physical Therapy was not your typical physical therapy practice. Most of the employees of the practice had been there for their entire careers, and the average tenure for the physical therapists was over 20 years. Although there had been some turnover, once someone joined the practice, he or she was like family. Steve was an exceptionally kind leader, oftentimes making decisions that other business leaders would not have made because he cared so much about the people who worked for him. This care and family-like culture translated to his patients as well. It was not uncommon for patients to request their doctors send them to Universal Physical Therapy, even if it cost them more, or if the location was inconvenient. Also, because of the long tenure of the employees, patients regularly came back with different injuries, and years later, had the same therapist who knew his or her name and remembered the last time he/she came to visit.

Steve knew that he wanted to focus on helping his patients when he started. It was this mentality that, unlike other practices, allowed him to survive all those years. At that point, his greatest source of referrals was other patients. They would comment to their friends and family about the care and kindness that they received at "Steve's place," not to mention the patient outcomes. Doctors loved sending patients there because they knew that their patients would get treated well, and most importantly, would have better health outcomes than from other practices. Some of the patient experiences that were above and beyond industry standards included: more one-on-one time spent with their physical therapist, being offered warm towels during therapy, seeing the same therapist for each visit, a guarantee of waiting no longer than 15 minutes in the waiting room, and generally just having a fun place to visit in the middle of a busy day.

The employees of Universal Physical Therapy were also very engaged. They were all happy to work there and viewed their team as a second family. Many had seen their children grow up together and go through life experiences together. They had been there for each other through the ups and downs of the business, and also each other's lives. This created a fun and relaxed atmosphere that was good for the employees, but also good for patients who felt this sense of family, and many came back for that reason alone.

The Physical Therapy Industry

As with any healthcare practice, many of the financials of Steve's practice were determined by insurance reimbursement rates. This meant, regardless of how much Steve charged for a particular service, the insurance companies decided how much he would be reimbursed. If he wanted to charge more, he could; however, that cost would be passed on to the patient. Steve was also competing with big, national physical therapy chains who had different reimbursement rates. Many of their rates were more than Steve was getting for the same service. The insurance companies also put rate caps on the services that physical therapy offices could charge. That meant that, even if Steve was getting a lower rate than another physical therapy practice, he could not charge the patient to make up for the difference. It also meant that he had to keep the rates at, or under, the rate cap for each insurance company. Steve knew that the insurance reimbursement rates were a hard issue for many of his patients to navigate. For that reason, he would have his front office employees call the new patients before their first visit, and explain exactly what would be covered by insurance and what he/she would need to pay out of pocket. This was unheard of in the industry; however, it was part of Steve's mission to treat patients like family and ensure that they had a great experience.

Unlike most doctors' offices, patients could only visit Universal Physical Therapy through referral. When Steve first started his business, the law stated that one had to be a licensed physical therapist in order to own a physical therapy business. At that time, he was competing with many other local physical therapy businesses, as well as the big hospital chains in the area. But since then, the regulations had changed, and anyone could open a physical therapy business. This meant that doctors started to embed physical therapy offices in their practices. For example, there might be an orthopedic surgeon who has one physical therapist on site, and refers all his/her patients to that one person, generating more revenue for the surgeon's office. Although this model might be more convenient for the patient, the typical doctor's office did not have the proper equipment or resources to effectively conduct physical therapy. Because of this change in the competitive landscape, it was very rare to find many small physical therapy firms like Universal Physical Therapy.

One unique difference in the physical therapy industry is the type of work each position performs. This delineation of responsibilities was most prevalent between physical therapists (PTs) and physical therapy assistants (PTAs). The physical therapist was a supervisor of sorts for the physical therapy assistants. One difference was the amount of time spent with each patient. A physical therapist would spend 45 minutes with a patient, while a physical therapy assistant would spend 30 minutes. A PT was the only position that could conduct a new patient evaluation, and a PTA could only take over after the PT had conducted the evaluation. Once the patient had been going to physical therapy for several sessions, the PT had to check in to make sure the treatment plan was working accordingly. If not, only the PT could change the treatment plan or method of treatment. PTs also had to sign off on the PTA's patient notes after each visit.

The industry was so prescriptive about roles and responsibilities that a physical therapy practice had to have a ratio of 1 physical therapist to 4 physical therapy assistants. If the ratio was greater than that, the practice could be out of the guidelines, and this would jeopardize the reimbursement rates and even their license.

Change in Educational Requirements

Since the business opened 40 years ago, the educational requirements to become a licensed physical therapist had also changed. When Steve was in school, the requirements were a five-year degree from an accredited institution. Since that time, the requirements had changed to a seven-year PhD. This meant that students needed to complete a science-focused, four-year undergraduate degree, and then go on for another three years to get a PhD in physical therapy. Previous graduates were grandfathered into the new model and did not have to go back to school for another degree.

Because of this change, the supply of Physical Therapists dropped and the market for new physical therapists grew tighter. Recruiting new employees took creative sourcing strategies and relationships. One avenue many physical therapy practices used were head hunters. While very expensive, head hunters could often find a few candidates that had the credentials needed and were willing to conduct initial interviews. Steve had tried online sites like Indeed and Monster; however, those candidates seemed to be gone before he could even schedule an interview.

Case Assignment

1. Although Steve was open to using a head hunter to find new physical therapists, he wanted to explore other options for how to source candidates. If you were hired as an external recruiting consultant, what advice would you give him? What recruitment sources would you suggest? What are the pros and cons to each?

2. If you were to design a recruiting assessment for Steve, what attributes, personality traits or skills would you include?

3. Are there any demographic characteristics that you would look for in a candidate? What "type" of candidate would you look for?

4. Using the resume summaries provided in Appendix 1, which candidate would you hire if you were Steve?

Quiz 2

1. **For our purposes, we can think about the recruiting process as a what?**

   a. Mobile phone

   b. Funnel with a filter attached

   c. Cooking pan

   d. Warm meal on a cold day

2. **What do assessments measure?**

   a. Someone's ability to wink with both eyes

   b. The success of our hiring process

   c. A person's future performance on the job

   d. Our ability to screen out candidates

3. **What is a construct?**

   a. A funny term for a site where a building is going up.

   b. A category that is measured using an assessment.

   c. Another name for an assessment

   d. No one has really defined it yet.

4. **When designing an assessment, you need to make sure that your criterion and _____ are related?**

   a. Hiring technology

   b. Hiring process

   c. Predictor(s)

   d. Assessment

5. **Since we use statistics to create and validate hiring assessments, it is important to remember what?**

   a. They are more scientific than we thought.

   b. They will inherently contain some error

   c. They are impossible to understand

   d. They are not worth using

6. **When we refer to "X, plus or minus some percentage" in our everyday vernacular, we are really referring to what?**

   a. Standard Measure of Error

   b. Validity

   c. Reliability

   d. Construct

7. **If an assessment has a reliability coefficient below .70, we would consider it to be what?**

    a. Excellent

    b. Good

    c. Meh.

    d. Of limited applicability

8. **Face validity measures what?**

    a. How far apart a candidate's eyes are apart from one another

    b. How well statistics can be used in the hiring process

    c. The extent to which the assessment appears to measure what it claims to measure

    d. If the person wears glasses or not

9. **What type of validity is at the "top" of the validation hierarchy?**

    a. Content validity

    b. Predictive validity

    c. Face validity

    d. Concurrent validity

10. Because we use statistics to create and validate assessments, there will naturally be some built in what?

  a. Fluff

  b. Bias

  c. Efficiency

  d. Accuracy

Solutions to the above questions can be downloaded from the **Online Resources** *section of this book on* **www.vibrantpublishers.com**

Appendix

Name	Josh	Jeff	Lauren	Sarah
Highest Education	Master's of PT, Oakland University, Michigan (1995)	Doctorate of PT, Andrews University, Michigan (1997)	Doctorate of Physical Therapy, Grand Valley State University, MI (2015)	Bachelor of Physical Therapy, Wayne State University (1989)
Work Experience	Staff PT – Beaumont Hospital (2011 – Present)	Staff PT – Henry Ford Health System (2007- Present)	Physical Therapist – Home Health Care (7/2018 – Present)	PT – McLaren Hospital (2003 – Present)
	Staff PT – Atlas (2009 – 11)	Staff PT – ATI Physical Therapy (2006 – 2007)	Physical Therapist – Heartland Health Center (9/2015 – 7/2018)	Home Care PT (2011 – 2013)
	PT Supervisor – FlexU Physical Therapy (2008)	Therapy Director – Concentra Health Group (2001 – 2006)	—	PT – PT Professionals (1994 – 2003)
	PT Supervisor – Top Notch Care (2007 – 2008)	Staff PT - Home Rehab (2004 – 2005)	—	PT- Macomb Hospital (1990 – 1994)
	Staff PT – HealthSearch Physical Therapy (2005 – 07)	Staff PT – Henry Ford Hospital (2003 – 2004)	—	—
	Lead PT – Oakland PT (1996 – 1999)	Staff PT – Sinai-Grace Hospital (1997 – 2003)	—	—
	Staff PT - Henry Ford Hospital (1992 – 1995)	—	—	—
Professional Development	Integrated Manual approach to Low Back Pain	Physical Modality Basics	Treatment solutions for arthritis and osteoporosis	CPR Training
	Mid-American Sports Medicine Certificate	Kinesio Taping	Parkinson's disease evidence-based treatment course	Total Spine Treatment course
	Investment Fundamentals for PT Practice	Rehabilitation with Cardiopulmonary Issues Rehabilitation intervention for neurological Diseases	—	Care of the cognitively impaired course
Extra-Curricular Activities	Coach – St. Clair Shores Redwings Hockey Team	Member – Detroit Rotary Club	Pro Bono Coordinator – Grand Valley PT Program	American Physical Therapy Association
	Treasurer – St. Clair Shores Boat Club	Member – Detroit Athletic Club	President – PT Association of Michigan	Michigan Physical Therapy Association

This page is intentionally left blank

Chapter 3

Total Rewards

The function of total rewards includes compensation and employee benefits. This is one area within HR that is ripe for opportunities for HR analytics to help make better decisions. This chapter will highlight some of those areas, and provide an overview of job evaluation, pay equity, salary surveys, benchmarking, incentives, evaluation of benefits programs, and metrics. There is also a case study at the end of this chapter to allow you to practice your skills.

Key learning objectives include the following:

- Understanding of the job evaluation process and a basic understanding of the steps involved

- Understanding of why organizations conduct salary surveys and benchmarking

- Understanding of how to use the salary survey data and benchmarking results to create a pay structure

- How to measure incentives

- How to evaluate benefits

- Applying the knowledge gained by completing the case study at the end of the chapter

3.1 Job Evaluation

One the most common questions that HR professionals hear is, "How much is this job worth?" This question can come up when negotiating with candidates for a job, creating new jobs or new organizational structures, or simply when someone asks for a raise. Although there are several ways to answer this question, the most methodological way to answer it is to do a job evaluation. This chapter covers only the basics of job evaluation, which will provide you with an analytical way to base answers to questions about the value of a job or a set of jobs.

The definition of job evaluation is the process of "systematically determining the relative worth of jobs to create a job structure for the organization" (Milkovich, Newman & Milkovich, 1996). The great part about a job evaluation is that it can cover several factors such as: content of the job, skills required, value to the organization, organizational culture, and external market. Taking all these different factors into consideration, we can assess the value that an organization has for a job. An important note about job evaluation: the same job may not be as valuable in one organization as it is in another.

There are several methods to job evaluation. This section will review them and then dive deeply into one of those methods to give you a basic understanding of how to conduct the job evaluation.

3.1.1 Ranking

The first method of job evaluation is ranking. This can be either a simple ranking of the jobs by their value, or a paired comparison, meaning jobs are compared to one another. In a paired comparison, participants are asked to look at two jobs and rank which one should be valued more within the organization. Ranking can be a cheap and fast way to evaluate a job; however, ranking is not free from considerations. One drawback is that a lot of work needs to be done to compare a few jobs. Because each job needs to be compared to all the others, the number of comparisons can be large. Also, the ongoing upkeep of this method can be hard to maintain as jobs change over time.

3.1.2 Classification

Classification is the second method used to conduct a job evaluation. In this method, each job is categorized into a classification, or broader job category, along with other similar jobs. Deciding the classification in which the job belongs requires experience and is a bit of an art form. Also, writing the classification to adequately describe the work detail, while allowing for generalizability across jobs, is a skill in and of itself. The job classification method requires years of experience and is not something that many organizations use.

3.1.3 Point Method

The third method of job evaluation is the point method. In the point method, an assignment of points is given to a job based on compensable factors. Those factors are numerically scaled and weighted to reflect the importance of each factor (Risher, Fay, Holley, & O'Connell, 1997). We will cover the point method as an example for using HR analytics to gain consensus, and align compensation strategy with organizational strategy.

Step 1: Job analysis.

We covered job analysis in a previous chapter, so we will not cover this in detail here.

Step 2: Compensable factors.

Compensable factors are those attributes of a job that are meaningful to the organization, and for which the organization will compensate its employees. In order to determine the compensable factors for any given job, we need to choose those characteristics that the organization values. We typically will ask ourselves, "What is it about this job that adds value to our organization?" We also then need to get leaders to buy-in based on business strategy, which can be a task in and of itself. Compensable factors should also reinforce organizational culture and working norms. They should be based on the actual work being done, which means that we need to review job descriptions and ask the people who are doing the job.

Pro Tip

When business strategy changes, compensable factors should be reviewed and aligned with that new business strategy.

Step 3: Determine the number of factors.

The next step is to determine how many factors we need in a compensation system. This is a question that has that age-old response of, "It depends!" Organizational culture, stakeholder management, and timeliness are often the determining factors for how many factors should go into a job. Several studies have been conducted about the influence of additional factors on the job evaluation results. Studies as far back as the 1940's show that the combination of the right factors can generally account for 98% to 99% variance in the outcomes of job evaluation (Lawshe, 1945).

Step 4: Scale and weight the factors.

The next step is to scale and weight the factors. In this step we determine the scales that reflect different degrees within each factor and weight the factors according to their importance. Typically, this is part of the process that is done by committee. In this step we are determining what weight each of the factors represents in the overall job. The total sum of weight should equal 100%.

Although it's not a technically difficult or heavily statistical method, using analytics to gain consensus, and help describe the thought process, can help make the next steps in the compensation process much easier.

3.2 Salary Surveys and Benchmarking

Provide compensation programs that are competitive within global financial services to attract the best talent to successfully execute the company's strategy. – **Citi Group**

Every year, we examine the compensation employees receive and make adjustments to ensure that we maintain pay equity. – **Apple**

> *We pay salaries that are designed to attract and retain superior leaders, and we pay annual bonuses to reward exceptional performance.*
> – GE

The pay philosophies listed above are taken from three of the world's best-known companies. We can see similarities in them, such as attracting and retaining good talent, reviewing compensation annually, executing or performing, etc. It is fine for a company to say these things on its website or SEC filing documents, but there is much more work being done behind the scenes to maintain these pay philosophies, and ensure that the organization is, in fact, attracting the best talent. The next section will highlight some of the ways that analytics can help in the design of a compensation system.

3.2.1 Salary Surveys

The salary survey is a systematic way for an organization to gather information about the compensation paid by other organizations. Organizations conduct salary surveys for various reasons. They may want to adjust pay levels of certain jobs, adjust pay mix, adjust pay structure or evaluation method, or attempt to estimate competitor pricing and cost.

Because a salary survey can be used in so many situations, we need to make sure we are comparing apples to apples when conducting our own salary survey and benchmarking. We need to compare the same skills, the same geographic area, and the same products or services being provided by the job. The importance of stakeholder management is critical at this stage of the process. Many decisions need to be discussed internally and with various stakeholders. Things like: how many jobs should be benchmarked? What companies to benchmark? How many companies to benchmark? How to use the data? What information to include? Total rewards? Just base salary? All these things need to be answered before embarking on a salary survey. The survey is then sent to various organizations for completion.

Once the surveys are completed, we need to interpret the results and use statistics to construct a market line. The first step is to verify the data. We look for anomalies in the data and ensure that the companies included are the ones we want to benchmark. We should look for companies that dominate the survey results. Are there outliers?

Step two is statistical analysis. We want to look at frequency distributions, measures of central tendency, such as mean, median, and mode, and we also want to look at variation. All these things are important; however, regression analysis can tell you the real story.

Step three is to conduct a regression analysis. A regression analysis, in this instance, allows us to create a market line. A market line is a way to visualize the distribution of external data (represented by competitor data from the pay survey), against internal data (evaluation points).

See Figure 3.1 for the regression line of best-fit for a set of sample data.

Figure 3.1   Regression Line

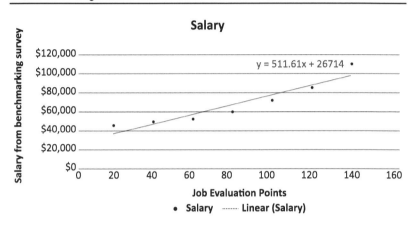

In order to create the market line, we can plot the results of the market survey on a simple scatterplot and use MS Excel to draw a regression line to create a market line (simply right click on one of the points on the graph and select, "Add trendline"). The market line tells us the line of best-fit for the data that we have in the chart. Excel can draw this for us very easily, and we can display the equation on the chart. We can use that equation to predict salaries of various jobs using market data. For example, using the figure above, a job with 40 job evaluation points would have a predicted salary of $47,178 (y = $26,714 + ($511.61*40)). This job has an actual salary of $49,000.

This method can be beneficial if you have a lot of jobs you need to synthesize and for which to determine a benchmark. Once the market line is determined, we have two pieces of the puzzle: the external view (salary survey data) and the internal view (job evaluation points). We can now move to creating a pay structure and pay bands within our organization. We will not cover that here, as this is not a compensation book; however, included in Figure 3.2 is what ranges might look like based on the regression line, or market line, that we have drawn with our salaries in Figure 3.1.

Figure 3.2   Potential Ranges based on Regression Line

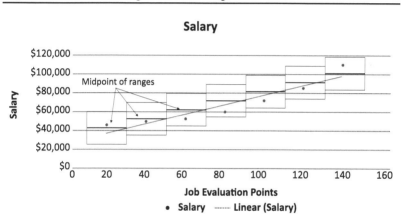

3.2.2 The Execution of a Salary Survey

Typically, organizations will conduct surveys in partnership with a consulting firm. There are many benefits to this approach, including the time it takes to conduct a survey of this nature, the independence of a third party, and contacts of potential participants, which are plentiful from a consulting firm. Interpretation of results is also important. Typically, consulting firms are best equipped for this task because they do this type of work all day every day. The final reason why most companies choose to outsource this process is that technology for data collection is part of the investment made by the consulting firm.

3.3 Incentives and Pay-for-Performance

Incentives can be used for several different reasons.

- Sales incentives can be used to change the selling behaviors of salespeople, as in from selling high-priced items to selling high-margin items.

- Long-term incentives can lead to longer retention of high-performing employees if done correctly.

- Incentivizing production workers by piece, as opposed to by hour, can incent faster production.

We must remember that with every decision about incentives, there are often unintentional consequences such as the following:

- Selling high-margin items may result in fewer overall sales.

- If the performance management system is biased, giving long-term incentives to the "high-performing" employees, it may incentivize the wrong people to stay.

- Faster production may result in more error, scrap, or rework.

Discussion Question:

In your experience do long-term incentives work?

Solution to the above question can be downloaded from the
Online Resources section of this book on **www.vibrantpublishers.com**

In order to understand the basics of pay-for-performance, we need to understand a bit about labor economics. There are many other texts worth a read that do a great job of explaining the basics of the economic theory of incentives, but we need to at least cover them briefly here to ensure that we are on the same page.

The basic model of agency theory is most applicable when dipping our toe into economic theories of incentives. In short, the agency theory explores the relationship between one party (called the principal) who delegates work to another party (the agent), who performs that work (Eisenhardt, 1989).

The agency theory tries to resolve two things. First, is the agency problem. The agency problem occurs when the desires and goals of the two parties are in conflict, and it is difficult for the principal to measure the activities of the agent. The agency theory also tries to resolve the problem of risk-sharing when the two parties have different attitudes toward risk.

The agency model assumes three things (Baron and Kreps, 1999). The first is that the employee is averse to effort, meaning that he or she will work as little as he or she can while still getting paid, if paid by unit of time. The second assumption is that the employee is averse to risk (especially his or her compensation that might be at risk due to pay for performance) and makes decisions about efforts based on this aversion to risk. The third assumption is that the parties cannot agree on the level of effort required for the job, therefore the principal should employ some type of monitoring, which is rife with issues. Monitoring can be hard to do, it can create cheaters, etc.

Maybe paying for output is the answer.

Discussion Question:

What are some issues that might arise if everyone was paid for output?

Solution to the above question can be downloaded from the
Online Resources section of this book on **www.vibrantpublishers.com**

There can be several issues with paying for output as well. For example, how would you measure the output of an HR manager? How would you ensure that the output is a direct function of the effort of the employee? What kind of monitoring would you need to do to ensure the quality does not suffer? What if output is hampered by the tools provided by the principal? How do you incentivize teamwork? Company culture? Etc.

There is no perfect system, and many economic theories assume that we are all "Homo economicus," meaning that we are all rational beings who are self-interested in optimally pursuing our interests. For a great read on examples that are clear deviations from being "Homo economicus," see Nudge and Misbehaving by Richard Thaler, or really anything about behavioral economics.

So, where does this leave us and how can analytics help?

First of all, the right incentive scheme depends on several different factors, such as the culture of the organization, desired outcomes, technology available to complete the task and monitor progress, teams necessary to complete the work, ability to measure outcomes versus effort, and how much ambiguity is in the task or outcome. With all these potential trade-offs, it's no wonder so many consulting firms have incentive compensation practices! From an analytics perspective, it is important to understand these trade-offs and then dive into the data and design experiment to see which incentives work, and which ones just look good on paper.

3.3.1 Measuring the ROI of Incentives

This process does not have to be complicated, however, it can be politically charged within an organization. If we set up control and experimental groups appropriately and get the right buy-in from the right stakeholders, analytics can help to influence incentives. A simple calculation for the ROI, or return on investment, of an incentive program can be described as the following:

(Incremental change in income - cost of incentive program) / cost of incentive program

Take the two examples below. Are they worth the investment?

Table 3.1   **Low Cost Incentive Plan**

Group	Widgets produced	Incremental widgets	Revenue per widget	Incremental revenue
Experimental	100	25	$1.00	$25.00
Control	75	N/A	N/A	N/A

Total cost of incentive plan = $12.00

Discussion Question:
Is the incentive plan worth it? Why or why not?

Solution to the above question can be downloaded from the
Online Resources section of this book on **www.vibrantpublishers.com**

3.4 Evaluation of Benefits

The vast realm of employee benefits is another area for much discussion and debate, none of which we will get into in this section. However, we will cover the importance analytics plays in evaluation of employee benefits, though we will not go deeply into benefit schemes or benefit design because that is simply not the topic of this book. Typical areas of focus-of-benefits are the following:

- Legally required benefits: which differ by region and country

- Discretionary benefits: those the employer chooses to provide to employees in order to create a more attractive value proposition

Because legally required benefits differ greatly across the world, we will use an example of a discretionary benefit to demonstrate how analytics can play a role in the evaluation of employee benefits.

I have worked with several companies that have spent an inordinate amount of money and time on discretionary benefits. Inherently, this is not a bad thing, but almost none of those organizations have asked the question of, "Do these benefits really make a difference?" Using analytics, we can tease out the impact of certain discretionary benefits to the organization.

Let's say that you are the benefits director of a law firm, and you are considering a large-scale implementation of a work-from-home policy. This new policy has already been rolled out in a pilot group, and you want to see if it has made a difference in average monthly billable hours. Watch the example below to see how to analyze these data.

Refer to the video **Evaluation of Benefits.mp4** in **Online Resources** section of this book on **www.vibrantpublishers.com**

Discussion Question:

Based on the video, would you roll out a work-from-home program more widely? What considerations will you make before doing so?

Solution to the above question can be downloaded from the **Online Resources** section of this book on **www.vibrantpublishers.com**

3.5 Metrics

There are several metrics we have discussed already in this chapter; however, others that many organizations use are as follows:

- Average compensation by grade / salary band

- Average compensation by tenure

- Compa-ratio (overall, by performance, by location, etc.)

- Benefits adoption

- Benefit utilization (health benefits)

- High cost benefit utilization

The definition of these metrics can vary greatly from organization to organization; therefore, we will not define them here.

Chapter Summary

◆ The total rewards function(s) uses data all the time for things like salary benchmarking and equity analysis.

◆ Job evaluation is an important aspect of the compensation function and provides a quantitative measure by which you can benchmark jobs.

◆ Incentives can be a very powerful tool to use when influencing employee behavior; however unintended consequences should also be considered.

◆ The return on investment of incentive programs is something that is not always considered; however should be reviewed to ensure that the incentive plan is worth the investment.

CASE STUDY:
Incentive Plan Return On Investment

The following case study will give you a chance to practice calculating the return on investment of an incentive program. Reference the "Measuring the ROI of Incentives" section of this chapter for a refresher, and example of how to complete the case.

Overview

Anderson had worked at Cell U Max for about five years. He started as an HR generalist right out of school and was grateful for the experiences that he had been able to gain in such a short time. After three years as an HR Generalist, he moved into his current role in the compensation department. He really enjoyed compensation and was interested in learning more. He was an up-and-comer in the HR function and really had a knack for understanding how compensation worked. His next project was going to put that to the test.

His next task was to create a compensation plan that would incentivize salespeople in the cell phone stores to sell more high-margin items. The company was going through a restructuring and had realized that the incentives did not align to the new behaviors that it wanted its employees to exhibit. Anderson oversaw the creation of the new incentive program that would align to the new business model of maximizing profit margin.

Cell U Max

Cell U Max was a national cellular phone chain that sold all different types of cellular phones, provided service for those phones, and sold several different types of cellular phone accessories. Throughout the years Sell U Max was quite profitable and had focused its salespeople on selling phones. After all, that is how Cell U Max made it big. It was one of the first companies to embrace cellular technology and market it to a broad population. Over the last several years competition had snuck into the market and Cell U Max was questioning whether it had the right structure. Its current line of thinking was to minimize the selling of hardware and, eventually, get out of the hardware business altogether. Instead, Cell U Max would focus on providing service which required less overhead and fewer deals with external hardware providers.

Current Sales Model

The current incentive plan at Cell U Max was set up to maximize the sale of cellular phones. After all, each cell phone cost approximately $850 compared to the average service call which was $400 and the average accessory which was $25. On any given month a salesperson would sell an average of eight phones, five service contracts, and 20 accessories. The average margin on a cell phone was 10%, service calls was 40% and accessories was 30%. Cell U Max's new model was attempting to maximize service contracts and the hefty margin that came with them. Anderson's project was the key to executing this new strategy.

New Incentive Scheme

Having been in his role for a couple of years, Anderson knew that he was going to have to run a pilot before he rolled out his new incentive plan to the entire organization. Luckily, he had several stores in which he could do this. Taking advice from his manager, selected five stores for which he changed the percentage of each employee's bonus. In the old model, the sales of phones, service and accessories was weighted the same (33.3% each) and the salesperson was awarded 3% commission on each item sold. In the new model, selling cell phones was weighted 20%, service contracts was 70%, and accessories were 10%. Having run the pilot, Anderson knew that, by changing the percentage of each employee's monthly bonus by those percentages, the incremental sales for cell phones would be an additional two phones, and an additional four service contracts. Surprisingly, the number of accessories sold did not change.

Using the data from the pilot, Anderson calculated the average monthly incremental revenue to the organization and the total average income per salesperson per month. Once he completed his analysis, he sat back in his chair and asked himself, "Is this the right incentive plan for what we're trying to accomplish?"

Case Assignment

1. What is the total sales revenue for Cell U Max, on average per month for each of the three items (i.e, phone, service, accessories)? What is the total incentive earned per month per salesperson overall?

2. Compare the average income per salesperson per month in the old plan versus the average income per salesperson per month in the new plan. What are the differences?

3. If you were Anderson, how would you design an incentive
   scheme to align with Cell U Max's new strategy of maximizing
   high-margin products?

Quiz 3

1. **Job evaluation is the process of what?**

   a. Determining what jobs are needed in the organization

   b. Carving out time for work/life balance

   c. The process of firing someone

   d. Systematically determining the relative worth of jobs to create a job structure for the organization

2. **Which of these is not a method of job evaluation?**

   a. Ranking

   b. Banking

   c. Classification

   d. Point method

3. **A salary survey is what?**

   a. A systematic way for an organization to gather information about the compensation paid by other organizations

   b. Something that should only be done once every 10 years

   c. The process by which the CEOs of multinational organizations are paid

   d. A governmental requirement

4. How often do incentives work?

   a. Always

   b. Sometimes

   c. Never

5. If using incentives, we should pay for what?

   a. Output

   b. Effort

   c. Teamwork

   d. It depends on the organization because each one is different with its own unintended consequences

Solutions to the above questions can be downloaded from the **Online Resources** *section of this book on* **www.vibrantpublishers.com**

Chapter 4

Training, Succession and Careers

This chapter will describe several aspects of how analytics can affect and measure training, individual development, and career planning. Specific topics to be covered will be competency modeling, training needs assessment, experimental design, training measurement, predictive modeling through multiple regression, career planning, and succession planning.

Each of these topics could be a textbook in and of themselves; however, the intent of this chapter is to give an overview of where analytics can play a role, and how we can help business leaders and individual employees make better decisions about training, development, and careers.

Key learning objectives for this chapter include the following:

- Understanding of how analytics can play a role in competency modeling

- Understanding how to use HR analytics to conduct a training needs analysis

- Knowledge of the Kirkpatrick model and how to measure training

- Knowledge of experimental design and how to set up an experiment using training measurement

- Knowledge and application of regression modeling and understanding causality vs. correlation

- Applying the knowledge gained by completing the case study at the end of the chapter

4.1 Competency Modeling

In order to understand competency modeling, we first need to understand the definition of a competency. A competency is defined as a measurable skill, attitude, or attribute that contributes to success in a particular job (Berger and Berger, 2011). Examples of competencies are things like teamwork, decision-making, communication, problem-solving, results orientation, etc. Each of these things can potentially be measured, and developed, if the organization has a good sense of what competencies are important and how to develop them. All too often, the answer from HR professionals for how to develop a competency is to conduct training. We will see in this chapter that training is one answer, but not always the right answer.

One very important thing to consider when developing a competency model is that competency models need to be built for each organization. Cultural nuances play a major role in how competencies are understood and how behaviors manifest themselves. For example, in one organization the competency of decision-making might look very different than another organization. If decision-making is very hierarchical in one organization, the expectation of those who are not in leadership roles may be to provide information to those leaders who are, in order to allow them to make the decisions. In another organization, decision-making might be very dispersed, therefore employees would be expected to make their own decisions and have accountability for doing so. These cultural norms and behaviors can, and do, play a major role in the creation and success of any given competency model.

Pro Tip

- Competencies need to be created in the context of a given organization.
- Competency models need to be revisited over time and updated accordingly.
- Start slowly with a leadership competency model, as technical models can very quickly become complex.

Another important aspect about competency models is that they need to be revisited over time as the organization changes. Organizations are very dynamic phenomenons, and so should their competency models be. As organizations go through changes in market pressure, product offerings, new services, etc., the competency model, and those competencies that are most important to an organization, will need to change in kind.

There are several ways competency models can be developed. With each of these methods, they can get very complicated and easily overdone. When developing a competency model from scratch, take it slowly and begin with leadership competencies. Technical competencies can also become very complicated, with many different levels of competence, so the process can be muddied very easily. Leadership competencies are easier to develop when applied to a broader group of the organization. In other words, more bang for your buck!

4.1.1 Organization of Competencies

Competencies are usually grouped together to form a competency library. A competency library is a listing of the various competencies within an organization. They are the behavioral anchors (simply, observable behaviors) needed in order to measure those competencies. For example, if an organization has a competency called "teamwork," behavioral anchors might be things like, "works well with others" and "rallies around a group of individuals."

Typically, the competency library is then used to define success profiles for various roles. A success profile is a listing of the competencies necessary to be successful in a job. Sometimes success profiles also contain things, like important skills or technical abilities that an individual might need to have in order to be successful on the job.

After the hiring process, competencies are used in training needs assessments to describe what success looks like in various roles. Training needs assessment will be discussed later in this chapter.

4.1.2 Creating a Leadership Competency Model

There are several different ways to build a competency library and each method has its pros and cons. The method of constructing the competency library is usually based on timing, cost, and resources available. Here is a general overview of a process where analytics can play a basic, but important, role in the creation of a competency model.

1. Create or purchase a competency library. The decision to make or buy one is completely dependent on the time available, skills available within the organization to develop a library, and the budget required. This decision will vary from organization to organization and will also depend on what the organization plans to do with the competency library once it is created.

2. If not already defined, define the organizational drivers. In other words, what are the drivers of success for this organization? What gives this organization the right to play and win within its market? Why do customers choose this organization? All these questions will help an organization to better understand itself and better articulate those things that are important. For example, a high-tech organization that develops software in New York City would likely have very different competencies than an old-school manufacturing company in the Midwest. Neither one is better than the other, but it is critically important to understand what competencies are important to each organization, and why and how those behaviors can be developed.

Table 4.1   Competency/Organizational Driver Matrix

	Deliver premium service to our clients	Create a culture of transparency	Be bold – honesty and integrity are critical to success
Political Savvy			
Customer Focus			

3. Map the competencies to the organizational drivers (see Table 4.1 for an example of a competency / driver matrix). We could do this several different ways. Each method involves the engagement of stakeholders within the organization.

   a. The first way is to send out a survey to organizational stakeholders. The survey could simply ask each participant to indicate whether or not they believe that particular competency is related to the organizational driver. A simple check mark, or "x" in the box, would suffice. The number of "x's" are then totaled in each of the rows which allows us to prioritize the competencies. One could imagine that the competency with the most "x's" would apply most broadly to the organization, and is therefore, the most impactful.

   b. The second way to map the competencies to organizational drivers is to interview people and ask them what they find important to the organization. The end goal is the same as the survey; however, one added benefit to interviews is that you can ask participants to expand on their answers or provide other commentary for why he/she answered a particular way.

c. The third and final way we will discuss in this chapter is a focus group. Focus groups are a way to gather a lot of anecdotal and qualitative feedback in a short amount of time. Like interviews, we would be able to ask for further explanation of any given answers; however, focus groups come with their own set of challenges, such as group think and potential domination of the conversation by only a few participants.

Although these techniques are not technically difficult uses of analytics, these approaches provide a foundation for a successful competency model due to a few factors.

- First, it allows stakeholders to follow the rationale for selecting various competencies. When we bring our stakeholders along the journey, they are more likely to buy into the end product and use the competency model when needed.

- This method also provides a logical method for why certain competencies are more important than others. Often during the implementation of a competency model, leaders and managers who were not involved in the process from the beginning have their own opinions about why and how each of the competencies are used. Using this method of creating the competency model allows for us to explain our logic and why each of the competencies were selected.

- It is also repeatable and scalable throughout the organization if other success profiles need to be created.

Competency modeling does not have to be a labor-intensive process. Depending on the needs of the organization, competency modeling can be simplified or made more complex by further drilling down into each of the competencies. Analytics can help us map competencies and organizational drivers, once established. As mentioned above, this process is not a very technical use of analytics, however it does provide for a logic-based mapping of those competencies and is often appreciated by business leaders. By using analytics when designing competency models, the HR function can add value and demonstrate strategic thinking.

4.2 Training Needs Assessment

Once the competency model is developed, it is not only used in hiring, but also in the development of individual employees. One approach that organizations use to develop competencies is to conduct training. As part of that process, we first need to figure out if training is needed and appropriate, what competencies need to be developed, and how should we best develop them. This is where training needs assessment starts.

A training needs assessment is a systematic process for determining the current aptitude of the organization in a given skill or competency, which is then compared to the desired state or organizational need.

See Figure 4.1 for an example of the comparison between organizational need and current capabilities.

Figure 4.1   Organizational Needs Assessment

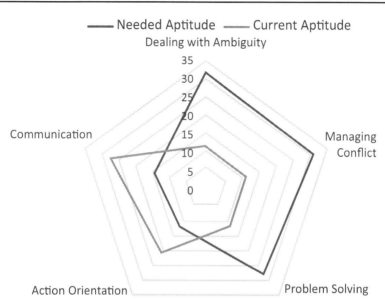

4.2.1 Why do we conduct a training needs assessment?

There are several reasons why an organization might conduct a training needs assessment. The first reason is to identify specific problem areas within the organization. These problem areas can then be addressed through training or other interventions, should they be necessary. Another reason to conduct a training needs assessment is to gain management buy-in into the process. (Further information about stakeholder management and how we can gather that throughout the process will be discussed later in this chapter.) The third reason to conduct a training needs assessment is to develop baseline data to use in an evaluation down the road. The final reason why we might conduct a training needs assessment is to determine the costs and benefits of training. With some assumptions, we can quantify how much training would cost, and compare that to how much it is costing the organization to not have the skills developed (Brown, 2002).

4.2.2 How to Conduct a Training Needs Assessment

There are several different ways to conduct a training needs assessment, all with the same objective: to determine the difference between the current level of competency or skill and compare it to that needed level of that competency or skill. The next step is then to determine if training is the right intervention to address the gap. A training needs assessment starts with gathering data. There are several ways by which we can gather data. It is always best to use more than one of these methods.

Organizational records

In many organizations, we can collect data each year on how individuals are performing in each competency or skill through an annual performance management process. Many organizations collect these data more than one time per year, which is even more helpful. We can use these data and the information in the HR information system in aggregate, to look across the organization and determine what skills or competencies are needed.

Personal interviews

Another method to gather data for training needs assessment is to conduct personal interviews. We talked about the role the analytics can play in the qualitative data gathering process in the previous chapter, and this is another great example of how we can use those skills to gather, organize, and analyze that qualitative data.

Focus groups

The third way that we can collect data for training needs assessment is by conducting focus groups. A focus group is simply the gathering of several individuals into a workshop in order to get a group perspective on a topic. There are pros and cons to this method. One benefit of this method is that you can collect a lot of data in a short period of time. However, one downside to this method is that you may have one or two individuals in the group who tend to dominate the conversation, not allowing for others to talk, or even influencing the thoughts of others.

Surveys

It is very possible that an organization might want to send a survey to several business leaders and employees about various competencies and skills that are needed. The surveys can be sent to different levels of the organization in order to collect a lot of data in a fairly short period of time. Surveys are typically less resource intensive and require less time to complete; however, unlike interviews or focus groups, we may not be able to get follow-up information if the surveys are anonymous.

Observations

Another common method to gather these data is to simply watch people do their job. For example, we could go to a shop floor and watch how employees conduct their job tasks, while taking lots of notes on what's going well and what needs to be further developed.

Once the data is gathered, we then need to perform the analysis to find the gap. The gap is the difference between where we want to be on a competency, and where we are today (see Figure 4.2).

Figure 4.2   **Organizational Needs Assessment Gap**

When the gap analysis is complete, we then need to decide if training is needed to address the gaps that are found. At this point, we are not sure the training is going to address the issue. For example, what if the issue is related to employee morale or lack of motivation? Training will not necessarily fix those issues; in which case we may need to research and implement other interventions such as mentoring or coaching.

Several factors will come into play when determining if training is the right solution such as things like cost, time, and resources to implement an intervention, the ability to design the right solution, delivery time frames, and return on investment. Because training is such a large investment of time and resources, it is very important to understand the benefits of that training before we suggest it as a potential solution.

If we determine the training will, in fact, address the issue at hand, we would then need to put together a proposal for training. A proposal could include the following: a summary of the gap analysis, the rationale for why we think training is important, a cost and benefit analysis, the timing needed to design and develop the training, and the budget required to do so. Oftentimes, this is where HR professionals stop. They conduct a training needs analysis and use analytics to determine the gap, then put together a proposal for why training is needed, and then they implement the training. The next step is measurement, which is the critical step in the end that many organizations fail to accomplish. Measuring the effect of training on the behaviors or competencies that were identified in the beginning of the training needs analysis is a critical step in the process. The next section will dive into experimental design and training measurement.

4.3 Training Measurement and Experimental Design

Oftentimes, HR professionals, with great intentions, try to fix problems quickly, without taking the time to determine how to measure the success (or not) of the intervention. It is critical, and one of the most impactful areas of HR analytics, to measure the success of a given training or development intervention. We use the term intervention because not every issue will be solved through training, just as discussed in the training needs analysis section. A very common method to use for training measurement is called the Kirkpatrick Model.

4.3.1 Kirkpatrick Model

This model was developed in 1955 by Donald Kirkpatrick. Although the model has since been debated and updated many times, it is still one of the most-used methods to evaluate the effectiveness of a training program. This model has four levels, each one adding more value to the business (Kirkpatrick and Kirkpatrick, 2006).

Reaction

This level measures the initial reaction of the training program from the learners. Learner sentiment is usually collected immediately after the training session via survey. Sometimes, in the field of HR, we call these "happy sheets." Some typical questions that you might see during this phase of evaluation would be, "Was the trainer knowledgeable about the topic area?", "Were the materials easy to understand?" Etc.

Learning

This phase of the model measures the amount of information, if any, that was absorbed by the participants. Typically, we measure this through the difference in scores between a pre-test and a post-test. In other words, participants would take a test containing content from the course that they are about to take. They would then take the course. Once the course is complete, that same test would be administered after the course. The "amount of learning" from the course is measured by calculating the difference in scores between the first and second tests.

Behavior

The next level is behavior change. This level measures if participants change their behavior(s) based on the training they took. This level can be difficult to measure. Typically, managers would rate their employees on a scale that shows whether they had changed the behaviors related to the course content after the taking the course, by observing when they are on the job. One hurdle to this method is inherent psychological biases from the rater, as they judge if there has been behavior change or not. For example, if an employee takes a course on "leadership," one manager might rate the demonstration of "leadership" very differently than another.

Results

Building upon behavioral change (both in terms of impact to the business and difficulty to measure), measuring the results, determines the result of the behavior change. This is the most difficult level to measure and is not often used by organizations because of the time and effort it takes, versus the information actually gained.

We can imagine that it is very hard to distinguish the cause-and-effect relationship of a training course as related to business results. Often, there are many confounding factors that come into play when trying to determine the cause of a business result. Market fluctuations, customer sentiment, cost of supplies, employee turnover, and process efficiency are just a few examples. Using experimental design and advanced analytics, we can get a better understanding of that relationship.

4.3.2 Experimental Design

Experimental design is an advanced method for determining the effect that an intervention has on measured behaviors. In other words, we are looking at how one thing affects another. We're trying to determine cause and effect. Please note: in this case, *trying* is the key word. We can never be sure that, especially when dealing with HR analytics and people, we have ruled out all extraneous variables from an experimental design. Just like a lab experiment in the field of chemistry, where we might manipulate one variable and measure the effect on another, we can try to do this in the field of HR.

There are two types of experiments. The first type is lab experiment. Lab experiments are conducted in a lab. This type of experiment is typically run under ideal conditions in order to study theories and new ideas in various fields. The second type of experiment is a field experiment. Although field experiments can be a little messier due to extraneous variables, they are usually more useful to practitioners. In both cases we're trying to determine the effect of one variable on another.

Pro Tip

We can never be sure that we have ruled out all possible confounding variables when conducting a field experiment.

4.3.3 External Factors

There are several external factors that could affect our experiment, especially if we do them in the field. Each of these should be considered and understood at the analysis stage of an experiment.

History effects

History effects are those things that happen during and outside of the experiment, which influence the outcome. An example of this would be sales training. If we were conducting an experiment on the effect of sales training and, at the same time, ran a nationwide add for a new product, we would not be able to isolate which had the bigger effect on increased sales. Was it the training or was it the advertisement?

Maturation effects

Maturation effects occur when the change in results of the pretest and the post-test are a function of the participants simply getting older (Maheux, B. and Béland, 1987). Examples of this occur when we conduct experiments in schools, because students tend to become more mature and develop further as they get older.

Testing effects

Testing effects are simply that the act of taking the pretest has influenced the results of the posttest (McDaniel, Anderson, Derbish, & Morrisette, 2007). For example, people who took the pretest know what things to look for and pay attention to in the experiment, and they score differently on the post-test because of it.

Selection bias

Selection bias is the selection of a group of participants that influences the results of the study (Hernán, Hernández-Díaz, & Robins, 2004). A classic example is using psychology undergraduates for psychological research. Do these results really generalize to the general population?

Mortality effect

This occurs when the results of the experiment are changed because people are no longer part of the study (Jurs and Glass, 1971). When we do field experiments within organizations, an example could be that some of the participants may have resigned and no longer work for the company. The lack of individuals can create an effect on the end results. This is called mortality effect.

Instrumentation effect

This could be due to the decrease of accuracy of the instrument over time, such as a micrometer that measures distance. In an organizational context, we might have a trainer observe some behavior, implement intervention, and then have a manager observe the final behavior. In this case the instrument (the trainer versus the manager) may have an impact on the results because those two different people interpret behaviors differently.

4.3.4 Training Measurement as an Experiment

In the field of HR, the measurement of training is a great example of a field experiment. Although we cannot necessarily control for all the variables, we can try to capture enough information to make some determinations about the effectiveness of the training offered. One way we can do this is using analytics. A common analytical technique used is called regression modeling. It is a great tool to use for isolating the effects of variables on one another.

4.4 Regression Modeling and Causality

In order to use regression modeling, we must determine a few attributes of two different elements. First, we need to determine if the factors are related. This can be done through a simple correlation. We then look at the correlation matrix between several different variables to see if they are related. The second step is to determine if one variable precedes the other. In other words, does one happen, and then the other one happens? Only after these first two steps are completed can we move on to the third step, which is ruling out other factors. Just because one variable comes before another and they are related doesn't mean that a third variable isn't influencing the first two. Therefore, we would typically use a multiple regression in order to isolate as many variables as we can that make sense in the model.

4.4.1 Multiple Regression

Multiple regression allows us to tease out those factors that have an impact on the variable that we are studying. There are several different types of regressions. We will only cover the basic regression model in this text. You can see the formula below:

$$Y = b_0 + b_1{}^*x_1 + b_2{}^*x_2 + b_n{}^*x_n$$

When we use a multiple regression, we're able to isolate the impact of our independent variables (x), on the dependent variable (y), while holding all other variables equal. In other words, we can tell which variables make the most difference on the change of our dependent variable. In the case of training, we can control attendance in a training class as well as other variables. If, through our analysis, we see that the training course has had a measurable impact on the dependent variable, we can confidently say that the training has had an impact.

Refer to the video **Multiple Regression.mp4** in **Online Resources** section of this book on **www.vibrantpublishers.com**

4.5 Analytics in Succession and Career Planning

Throughout my career, I've seen the results of many exit interviews and exit surveys which are given to employees who decided to leave the organization. The most common reason people leave an organization, across the world, is that they do not see an opportunity for career advancement. Even if 50% of those people are not telling the truth and left for another reason, career movement is an important aspect of an organization that should be understood.

4.5.1 Analytics in Career Planning for Individuals

Historically, when an employee would want to learn about a potential next move in his or her career, he or she would ask a boss or mentor. This can lead to all sorts of issues, most notably the tendency that we have biases that lead us to advise others to have a similar career path as ourselves. "It worked for me, so it should work for you, right?" Maybe.

In today's organizations, there is usually not a single way to get to a career level. Organizational structures change, competency models and needed skills change, jobs change, and employees need to be able to adapt their career path to the changing dynamics of the organization. Using analytics can help individual employees better understand the dynamics and consequences (both good and bad) of job movement. See Figure 4.3 for an example of a career map. You can see that this employee moved up, down and sideways through various functions.

Figure 4.3   Career Map Example

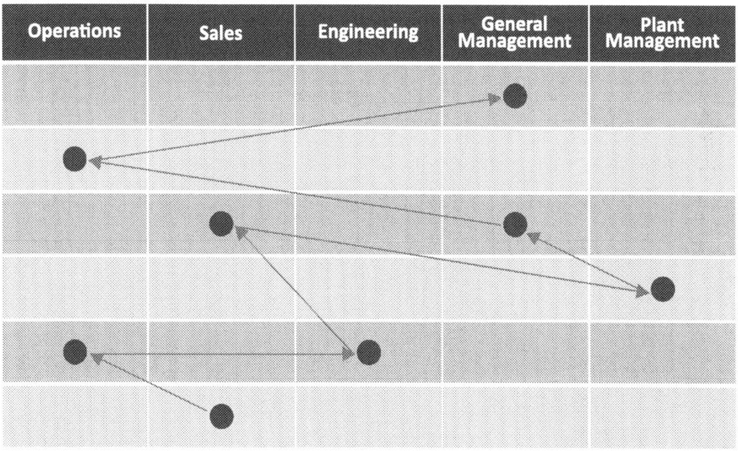

Organizationally, it is important to understand how people are moving into, within, and out of an organization. Simple career maps can help HR professionals understand the flow of labor within an organization. It is often very beneficial, even in the simple chart, to see the progression of one's career. When done using multiple people, we can see the macro trends and the flows of talent which can give us a good place to start conversations about how people move within the organization. We can then look at policy decisions and other recommendations based on current movement versus desired outcomes. For example, if we see that there is a glass ceiling for women, or that ethnic minorities "top out" at a certain level, we can start the conversation about why that might be the case.

4.6 Succession Planning

Succession planning is the process many organizations go through to ensure that the senior- most leaders have replacements ready for their positions. This movement of individuals could be due to promotions, job changes, or attrition of talent. The main objective of the succession process is business continuity. For example, if the president of a division were to retire, it would be very important for an organization to have someone ready to step into that role very quickly to ensure that the business can continue to run smoothly.

Typically, the succession process happens one time per year. During this time, the HR team sits down with business leaders to discuss potential successors for their roles. Although the terms may differ from organization to organization, the successors are usually rated on a time-based scale of readiness (e.g., ready now, ready in 1-2 years, or ready in 3 or more years). This process can take a lot of time and can be very labor intensive. Once a list of names is drafted, that list is typically vetted and validated with other business leaders. This process is called calibration.

During the calibration sessions, business and HR leaders are given the opportunity to weigh in on each successor and potential development options for those individuals. The calibration process can also take a lot of time and effort based on how many people need to be discussed, and at what levels the process needs to occur. You will have the opportunity to use this knowledge of succession planning and the regression skills from above in the case study that follows this chapter.

Although the measures listed thus far can be a good use of analytics, analytics can play a bigger role in the succession planning process. Using historical data and regression analysis, we can start to determine what aspects of the employment relationship are important to someone being on a succession plan. The case study at the end of this chapter will give you experience with using predictive analytics in succession planning.

4.7 Metrics

There are many aspects of the process that can be monitored and measured. We can break them up into two categories – process measures and pipeline measures. Some potential metrics are the following:

- **Process measures**

  - Number of roles filled from succession plans

  - Number of external hires for succession eligible roles

  - Recruiting costs for succession eligible roles vs. other roles

  - Development of individuals on succession plans

- **Pipeline measures**

  - Health of the pipeline for a given role

  - Diversity of the pipeline

  - Movement of successors

  - Flight risk of incumbents

Chapter Summary

◆ Many HR professionals do not think about measuring the impact of training or using analytics to help manage careers; however, this chapter has demonstrated how to do just that.

◆ Competency modeling is an important step in the training process upon which training content should be built.

◆ Training needs assessment is an important process to ensure that the training that is being designed is fulfilling a need in the organization.

◆ Kirkpatrick's Model is one way to effectively measure training.

◆ Experimental design can be used in training measurement to rule out other compounding factors that may affect the training outcomes.

◆ Regression modeling is one of the most powerful technical tools available in analytics.

◆ Succession and career planning are areas that are ripe for analytics; however many organizations do not take advantage of analytics in these areas.

CASE STUDY:
ManuCo Succession Planning

Overview

The application of statistical methods (i.e., regression modeling) can be a very important tool to use in HR analytics. This case study will follow Charlotte, an up-and-coming talent management professional, as she navigates the annual succession planning process at ManuCo. You will then use techniques from the previous chapter to conduct a regression analysis for the succession planning process.

Background

It was that time of year again and ManuCo was getting ready for their annual succession planning process. Their head of talent management, Charlotte, was preparing to conduct a series of meetings with ManuCo's business leaders and HR Directors. During these conversations, Charlotte asked the business leaders about their current position, if any of the roles and responsibilities of the job had changed in the last year, and who they thought might be a good successor for their position, should that business leader move into a new role. Each year this was a monumental task and represented a sizable portion of the work of the HR organization. In addition, an HR director would meet with the business leader prior to his or her the meeting with Charlotte to discuss potential candidates for the succession pool. These conversations occurred over the course of several weeks due to scheduling, availability, and simply the ability for business leaders to identify people who they thought could fill their shoes.

After the initial meeting with the business leader, the HR Director and Charlotte would work together to draft a succession plan for that business leader. In some organizations, this meant going through years of profile data for each of the individuals who were proposed, validating types of experience, job history, performance history, etc. The process of putting together the actual succession plan took another several weeks.

The goal of this process was for each business leader's succession plan to roll up to the President of the business who would then conduct a calibration meeting with the other business leaders. This gave all leaders the ability to weigh in on potential successors and provide feedback to finalize the succession plans. After the daylong calibration meeting, the president of the business would take the finalized succession plans to the CEO for her approval. Once the CEO approved the plans, they would typically sit in a binder, on the shelf, until a position came open. At that time, the succession plan may or may not be reviewed and used to fill the open position.

There must be a better way

This year, Charlotte decided that she was going to do things a little bit differently. Based on her knowledge of predictive analytics, Charlotte decided to enlist the help of the human resources analytics department to conduct an analysis that might help predict succession pools. The intent of this project was to cut down on the amount of time that it took to create develop, draft, socialize, update, and finalize succession plans. This seemed especially important since they were not being used or reviewed on a regular basis.

Charlotte sat down with the head of HR analytics, Linda, to determine what the project steps might be if they were to conduct an evidence-based succession planning study. Linda informed Charlotte that before any work was started, they needed to put together a project charter and project plan. The project charter consisted of several elements that were going to be very important to the project. The project plan would include a timeline for all the activities they needed throughout the process and due dates assigned to each. Charlotte agreed and told Linda the rest of the background on why she wanted to conduct such an analysis. Charlotte then went back to her desk to draft a project charter and project plan.

Charlotte found the exercise of drafting the project charter very helpful, allowing her to think about what questions she was really trying to answer. She provided some background information about the issue as well as the deliverables that she expected. She also came up with a list of questions she wanted answered throughout this project. Those questions were as follows:

- What attributes contribute to someone being on a succession plan?

- What attributes detract from someone being on a succession plan?

- Can we predict "good" successors based on attributes of individuals?

- Is there a difference between 'good' and 'bad' successors in each of our business units?

Although she knew these were many questions to address in one project, Charlotte decided to draft the project charter and bring it back to Linda. Charlotte also drafted a project timeline.

In her timeline she had accounted for the collection of data, both qualitative and quantitative, the cleaning of the data that Linda's team would help with, performing the analysis of those data, and finally putting the presentation together. All said and done, Charlotte projected, based on previous work she had done with Linda and her team, that this project would take approximately four months to execute from start to finish.

Interviews

Once Charlotte reviewed the project charter and timeline with Linda, she was eager to get started. She needed to engage the HR leadership team in this project because, ultimately, they would be the users of the final product in whatever form it took. After talking to Linda about the possibilities of predictive analytics, Charlotte then conducted analyses that would identify important attributes of individuals on succession plans, as well as, potentially, an algorithm that could predict the probability of someone being on a succession plan.

With this goal in mind, Charlotte set out to collect anecdotal feedback. The anecdotal feedback would be obtained via face-to-face interviews. Knowing that the HR function was the main customer for this analysis, Charlotte made a list of people she wanted to interview. The list included a representative sample of HR Directors and HR Managers from across the enterprise. Charlotte was confident this group of individuals would give her the anecdotal information that she needed to help guide her analysis. She then knew if she were able to speak with the individuals on that list, they would give her a good sense of the succession planning process—the good, the bad, and the ugly. Charlotte started scheduling interviews straightaway.

The first hurdle

Two weeks later, Charlotte realized that scheduling interviews with these stakeholders would be harder than it first seemed. She spent two weeks trying to get in front of the stakeholders. Some of them simply were not available or did not want to be available. Although she knew scheduling would be a challenge, she had no idea the extent to which this was a roadblock. Not wanting to slow down, Charlotte started to do some research on her own. Thanks to internet research, Charlotte was able to find several articles on succession planning; however, most of them were related only to the process. Very few were related to potential attributes of good successors. Not getting discouraged, Charlotte reached out to her network to see if her colleagues at different companies could help. After speaking with several directors of talent management at other companies, Charlotte realized one thing about succession planning—the results of the succession planning process really depend on the organization and its internal values. As she was talking to one of her team members about her findings, she remarked, "As the leader of an organization, you would logically want to pick someone who represents the values you bring to the table and that are also important to the organization." With her new knowledge in hand, Charlotte started the interviews with the HR directors within ManuCo.

Feedback

Although Charlotte heard many different attributes that may lead to someone being on a succession plan, several themes emerged from her interviews. One theme she heard about was tenure within the organization. Several of the HR directors cited that an individual had to be in the organization at least five years before even being considered for a succession plan. A few of the

HR directors thought that the needed tenure should even be as long as 10 years before being considered for a succession plan.

The second theme Charlotte heard was the need to be able to manage a group of others before being considered on a succession plan. Charlotte's working theory behind why this might be important was twofold. First, someone needed to be at a high enough level in the organization to manage people, and therefore in an eligible position to be a successor to a senior leader. Also, Charlotte hypothesized that the organization valued people leadership and the passing of organizational values down to future leaders. This was another theory she would have to test with this project team.

The third theme was performance. Charlotte heard from several of the HR directors that in order to be on a succession plan, the individual must have had great performance (a rating of 8 to 10, based on a 10-point scale) in the year prior. Many of the HR Directors even commented that their business leaders often confused performance with potential when planning for successors to their positions. This was a sticking point throughout the organization and something that Charlotte wanted to explore.

Analysis

Because Charlotte had done some preliminary research, both inside the organization and with external sources, she determined the best type of analysis would likely be a regression model. Charlotte thought that multiple regression analysis would provide enough information to be able to tell which of the variables made a difference, as well as not over-complicating the analysis. She had learned about regression in school and was familiar with how to conduct one while maintaining data integrity and coming to reasonable conclusions.

The first step in the analysis was to define and gather the data. Charlotte decided to include the following variables in her analysis:

Tenure

The first variable Charlotte decided to include was based on her interviews. Tenure was defined as the number of years an employee had been with ManuCo. She calculated this variable by subtracting the employee's start date from the date on which she ran her analysis.

Number of years in mentor program

The second variable Charlotte decided to include was the number of years in ManuCo's mentorship program. ManuCo had set up a mentorship program that matched high-performing employees with senior leaders. Each pair would meet on a regular basis for 12 months to help guide the employee and serve as a champion for that employee and his or her career interests. Participants were selected by the HR Directors and business leaders, and everyone spoke very highly about their participation. Year after year, this was heralded as one of the best programs that the HR function championed. The program was 10 years old and, at this point, some of the mentees had become mentors. For that reason, Charlotte decided to include total number of years in the mentorship program, both as a mentee and a mentor. This variable was calculated by simply counting the number of years each employee had participated in the program.

Age

Charlotte also decided to include the variable of age. This variable would serve as a proxy for general work experience, meaning that if someone joined ManuCo in the middle of his or her career, Charlotte would be able to capture his or her other work experience through this variable. This method is common in labor economics research, and Charlotte decided to include it in her model. In order to obtain these data, Charlotte ran a simple report from the HR information system which housed employee data.

Performance

Another variable that Charlotte decided to include was the most recent performance rating. ManuCo had a very detailed performance management system and rated employees on several different aspects of performance. These individual ratings were then aggregated into an overall performance metric. That overall metric was based on a 1 to 10 scale (1 = worst, 10 = best). Ratings were calibrated among leaders at the end of the year to ensure fairness and relative ranking among employees. These data were gathered through the performance management system, and Charlotte merged them with her original data set.

Average number of years in role

The final independent variable that Charlotte decided to include was the average number of years each employee served in each role they held at ManuCo. This variable would serve as a proxy for job movement. In other words, if someone had a low number of average years in role, that meant that he or she potentially had several roles at ManuCo. If an employee had a long average time in a role, that would signify that the employee did not change jobs very often. This variable was operationalized by calculating the time and role for each employee and averaging them throughout his or her tenure with ManuCo. Although there might be some "noise" in this variable, due to some employees having lower tenure resulting in lower average time in a role, Charlotte considered this and made the decision to include this variable anyway.

Outcome variable

In order to predict the number of succession plans a particular employee might be qualified for, Charlotte decided to use number of succession plans in a given year as her dependent variable in the regression equation. Although this took a lot of work, Charlotte and her team counted the number of succession plans on which each employee was included.

Case Assignment

Using the data provided (download predictive succession data), conduct a regression analysis in Excel to determine the predictors of the number of succession plans for which a particular employee might be qualified. Please consider the following:

1. The results of your analysis.

2. Your thoughts on potentially writing an algorithm to predict individual results. Should we do it? Shouldn't we? Why or why not?

3. Potential programmatic changes that ManuCo could make to address your findings.

Please note: if you haven't already, you may need to install the Excel "Data Analysis" Toolpak. You can find simple instructions online for how to do this.

Quiz 4

1. **What is a competency?**

   a. A part of a supercomputer

   b. Something that only front-line leaders need to understand

   c. A measurable skill, attitude, or attribute that contributes to success in a particular job

   d. A standard of analytics as described by the Association for HR and People Analytics

2. **Which is not a method to gather data during a training needs assessment?**

   a. Interviews

   b. Observation

   c. Surveys

   d. Guessing

3. **Which is not a part of the Kirkpatrick model?**

   a. Reaction

   b. Results

   c. Behavior

   d. Personality

4. **When conducting a field experiment, we can never be sure to account for all of what?**

   a. Rainfall that year

   b. Internal variables

   c. External factors

   d. The work that needs to be done

5. **What is the first step in regression modelling?**

   a. Determining if our variables are related

   b. Dumping our data into a statistical software

   c. Reach for this book

   d. Cry

6. **When conducting a regression model, we are trying to determine the impact of our independent variables on what?**

   a. Our external factors

   b. Our internal factors

   c. Our assumptions

   d. Our dependent variable

7. **Although a good idea in theory, using data to do individual career planning is not advisable.**

   a. True

   b. False

8. **Succession planning is** _____.

   a. The annual process that some organizations use to ensure business continuity

   b. Pointless

   c. Something too complex to use analytics

   d. The 8th wonder of the world

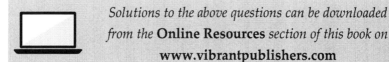

Solutions to the above questions can be downloaded from the **Online Resources** *section of this book on* **www.vibrantpublishers.com**

Chapter 5

Nonexempt Workforce

Although many of the analytical techniques and scenarios discussed before this chapter could apply to the nonexempt workforce, most of them are only used with data from the exempt workforce. While many reasons for this are driven by organizational culture, the nonexempt workforce can be a great source of insight for an organization. Using analytics can help us to better understand this part of the employee population.

Key learning objectives include the following:

- Understanding a typical hourly workforce hiring process and how to apply analytics

- Understanding of how to conduct a utility analysis for the hiring process, especially for the hourly workforce

- Knowledge of how to use analytics in the collective bargaining process and other negotiations

- Using knowledge gained to better assess absenteeism

- Applying the knowledge gained by completing the case study at the end of the chapter

5.1 Why focus here?

When it comes to the nonexempt workforce, the potential for analytics is limitless. Here are a few reasons why:

- Many times, there is higher turnover in the nonexempt workforce, giving us more observations to incorporate into our studies.

- It is also easier to quantify productivity in many cases. For example, quantifying the productivity of a production worker would be much easier than quantifying the productivity of an HR manager.

- Sometimes, it is easier to rate performance based on that productivity. The ease of measuring performance often depends on how the performance is defined, for example, measuring team performance, versus individual performance, versus plant performance, and so forth, etc.

- Another reason why the nonexempt workforce can be easier to analyze is because experiments can readily be designed and executed to conduct studies more efficiently, such as, assigning employees to various control groups, versus experimental groups, which then allows us to conduct studies more efficiently.

- The final reason is that often the nonexempt jobs are not as specialized as the exempt workforce. By creating similarities in the type of work from employee to employee, an optimal environment is created under which we can conduct a study.

Discussion Question:

What areas of the nonexempt workforce do you think would be best suited for analysis?

Solution to the above question can be downloaded from the **Online Resources** section of this book on **www.vibrantpublishers.com**

5.2 Hourly Hiring

In many companies, one of the main tasks for an HR manager is to hire hourly employees. Due to the quantity of people who apply for a given job, many opportunities can be used to maximize the hiring process. Unfortunately, this is also one of the most common processes that is outsourced to a third party. Many companies spend millions of dollars every year on third-party vendors to hire hourly employees. They set up assessment centers, take employees off the line to help administer the assessments, and take up space in the plant for physically setting up the assessment.

Because so much time and effort are spent on hourly hiring activities, it is critical for companies to understand how their hourly employees are being hired, and what aspects of the process are being measured. In terms of validity and reliability, all the same principles apply from the recruiting chapter of our book; however, those things become even more important because of the quantity of hires and applicants that companies usually have for their hourly positions. One way to ensure that the right process and outcomes are being used is to conduct a utility analysis.

5.3 Utility Analysis

One helpful piece of the staffing process for anyone who is evaluating assessment tools, is to conduct a utility analysis. There are several different models which serve a purpose, though some are more refined than others. At the end of the day, the utility analysis can be most beneficial to HR practitioners because it quantifies, in monetary terms, the potential payoff of one assessment tool over another. This is a great way to communicate the benefits and drawbacks of an assessment with managers and leaders. The following is a model that will be demonstrated in this text (Schmidt, Frank & Hunter, John & McKenzie, Robert & Muldrow, Tressie, 1979).

The expected monetary gain from selection =
$N_s r_{xy} SD_y Z_x - N_T(C)$ where the following are true:

- Expected monetary gain from selection = the return to the organization for having a valid selection program, versus one that is not valid.

- N_s = number of job applicants selected.

- r_{xy} = validity coefficient of selection procedure.

- SD_y = standard deviation of work performance in dollars. Note: Based on previous research, we can assume that SDy is roughly 40% of the average salary paid for the job (Schmidt et al., 1979).

- Z_x = average score on the selection procedure of those hired expressed in z or standardized score form, as compared to the applicant pool (serves as an indication of the quality of the recruiting program).

- N_T = number of applicants assessed with the selection procedure.

- C = cost of assessing each applicant with the selection procedure.

Let's take a look at an example of when a utility analysis could be helpful.

 Refer to the video **Utility Analysis.mp4** in **Online Resources** section of this book on **www.vibrantpublishers.com**

5.4 Collective Bargaining

Collective bargaining is an area of HR and labor relations which does not get much attention from an advanced analytics perspective. On one hand, there are a lot of analytics from a financial perspective, such as creating costing models, calculating the current and future labor costs based on the outcomes of the bargaining, calculating the cost of various solutions, etc. But on the other hand, this is often where organizations (both union organizations and companies) stop short. Finances are often the primary concern when bargaining. In other words, how much will the agreement cost?

Imagine if, using analytics, we could identify a solution that is cost-effective for the company, beneficial to the employees, and makes the union happy. Win, win!

The bargaining process contains multiple steps (Budd, 2010). Analytics can help with many of those steps in ways some organizations do not consider. Each side needs to determine the following:

- First, they need to determine their interests or what they care about. These are the drivers of the bargaining strategy and the positions that the company and the union will take at the bargaining table.

- Second, each side needs to determine the options for those interests and conduct cost modeling associated with those options. It is not uncommon for both the union and the organization to conduct extensive cost modeling; that helps to better understand the future state of costs if the various options are agreed upon.

- Third, legitimacy is important to establish. Legitimacy is the external pressure each side uses to attempt to convince the other side that their offer is fair. For example, the union might use the current standard of living as evidence showing that employees need higher wages, while a company might use the average total cost of benefits to justify employees paying more for their benefits.

- Fourth, each side needs to determine the interests of the other side, or at least have a reasonable idea of the others' interests. Not only will this help with the "going in" positions, it will also help drive the conversation to a point of agreement.

Finally, each side needs to determine the best alternative to a negotiated offer; specifically, "What is our option if we cannot reach a negotiated offer?" Many times, this could be a strike. The good news??? Analytics can help with all these things!

So often, the interests of the company are determined by past experiences and anecdotal evidence, such as the number of grievances due to a specific part of the contract, issues in the local plant, etc. What if analytics could be used to determine what really matters (e.g., through regression analysis)? Better yet, what if we discover that what really matters to the company, is also desired by the union?

Win, win!

Let's play out an example.

On one side is the union; on the other is company management. (While this is a "typical" negotiation in the United States, you could potentially substitute a works council, or other organized labor organizations in other parts of the world). Table 5.1 shows the "going in" positions for each side of the negotiation. These are the positions each side takes into the very first meeting before the analysis is completed.

Table 5.1

Union "Going in" Positions	Management "Going In" Positions
Wants a 5% increase in profit sharing (from 4% to 9%)	Cannot afford more profit sharing
Wants additional training	Cannot afford to take employees from off the line for training
Wants stronger benefits	Wants to share a greater portion of the benefit cost with employees
Wants more vacation days	Wants to minimize the cost of the contract while maximizing profit margin

Does it seem there might be a bit of an impasse here? If the union heard from its members that they want more profit sharing, additional training, stronger benefits, and more vacation days, but the company cannot afford any of those things, and has the objective to minimize the cost of the future contract, one of the sides needs to give-in, right? Or do they?

Let's say the management side has a whiz bang analytics team behind the scenes who can take employee data and make some sense of it. (I use the management side because, in many cases, there may be legal issues in sending employee data to an external party, in this case, the union. The union could also have a whiz bang analytics team.) The analytics team decides to run a regression analysis to determine the impact of each of the union demands on profit margins. They are using data at a plant level because the company measures profit margin at a plant level. There are 10 plants in the company and the team decided to look at 5 years of data, resulting in 50 observations. The results of the regression analysis are below.

Figure 5.1

	A	B	C	D	E	F	G	H	I
1	SUMMARY OUTPUT								
2									
3	*Regression Statistics*								
4	Multiple R	0.97943734							
5	R Square	0.959297503							
6	Adjusted R Square	0.954672219							
7	Standard Error	0.70750739							
8	Observations	50							
9									
10	ANOVA								
11		*df*	*SS*	*MS*	*F*	*Significance F*			
12	Regression	3	519.0950649	103.819013	207.4029525	2.04989E-29			
13	Residual	44	22.02493512	0.500566707					
14	Total	49	541.12						
15									
16		*Coefficients*	*Standard Error*	*t Stat*	*P-value*	*Lower 95%*	*Upper 95%*	*Lower 95.0%*	*Upper 95.0%*
17	Intercept	1.682066165	0.662455608	-2.539137936	0.014723332	-3.017157717	-0.346974613	-3.017157717	-0.346974613
18	Average number of technical training hours	0.295437757	0.028148803	10.49557097	1.47161E-13	0.238707573	0.352167941	0.238707573	0.352167941
19	Average percent shared benefit cost	-0.126283803	0.047984734	2.631749555	0.011669506	0.029576926	0.222990681	0.029576926	0.222990681
20	Number of days off	0.157267019	0.072651422	-2.164679168	0.035878873	-0.303686339	-0.0108477	-0.303686339	-0.0108477

There are several things we should draw attention to in the output of the regression analysis.

- R Square (.95929): This explains the amount of variance in the dependent variable (profit margin) that is explained by the overall model. In other words, it describes how "good" our model is. Note: in the "real world" you will likely never see an R Square value this high.

- ANOVA table – *Significance F* (2.0498E-29): This tells us the statistical significance of our model. If the *F* value is below 0.05, our model is statistically significant. In our case, the *F* value is far below that.

- Coefficients: These are the "weights" for each of our independent variables. They describe the relationship between a "one-unit increase" in the independent variable and the impact to the dependent variable. Look at the interpretation below to get a better sense of how these can be applied to our example.

Table 5.2

	Coefficients	Interpretation
Intercept	1.682066165	This represents the expected mean profit margin if all the independent variables are zero.
Average number of technical training hours	0.295437757	For every additional average technical training hour per employee, the profit margin will increase by .2954. That's quite a commercial for technical training!
Average percent shared benefit cost	-0.126283803	For every additional average percent of shared benefit cost per employee, the profit margin will decrease by 0.1262. The company might want to rethink its strategy of benefits cost sharing!
Number of days off	0.157267019	For every additional average day off per employee, the profit margin will increase by 0.157. Maybe giving more days off is not such a bad idea after all???

- P-Values: Similar to the F statistic above, the P-values tell us if the results are statistically significant. The cutoff value is the same as the F statistic (0.05 or below). In our case, this means that the result for all our variables is significant. This very rarely happens in the real world.

Based on the results of the analysis, the company can revisit its bargaining strategy. For example, if we now know that additional technical training hours (a union demand) will increase profit margin (a company goal), and some of that additional profit margin can be shared with employees (another union demand), the company might want to propose that every employee attend technical training. This solution not only addresses two union demands, but also ensures that the company is meeting one of its main goals of increasing profit margin. Win, win!

This is a very simple example with fictitious data. These data do not exist as cleanly in the real world as they do in a book. However, I hope that you have seen the value that analytics can bring to the bargaining table. Much of the time, bargaining can become emotional, and each side can become entrenched in its position. The use of analytics can (hopefully) break some of that tension and make for more productive bargaining, and ultimately, better relationships between the company and organized labor unions.

5.5 Productivity Analysis

As it relates to the nonexempt workforce, the golden question in many executive minds is, "What makes our workers more productive?" On average, the time for new hires to achieve full productivity ranges from eight weeks for clerical jobs, to 20 weeks for professionals, to more than 26 weeks for executives (Williams, 2003). For many years, the productivity question has clearly been on the minds of many executives and managers throughout the world.

The notion of productivity analysis started with the classic example of the Hawthorne effect. The Hawthorne effect was established at Western Electric's Hawthorne Illinois facility. Several industrial engineers set out to determine how to make workers more productive through evidence from scientific management theory (Gale, 2004). They set out to study the effect of environmental change (specifically lighting) in a social setting, in this case the workplace. They started by brightening the lights and found that productivity went up. They then dimmed the lights. Sure enough, productivity also went up.

The main finding of these studies was that teams are more productive when they have input into their work environment, and when they feel that someone cares about their working conditions. Some evidence suggests that the Hawthorne effect is not real (Levitt and List, 2011). However other evidence suggests that there might be some truth to the theory, but more research is needed (McCambridge, Witton & Elbourne, 2014).

Regardless of the outcome or legitimacy of the Hawthorne Effect, it is a perfect example for conducting a field experiment and gathering data in a "real-world" environment (something that you learned about earlier in this book!). Hopefully, you now have the necessary tools to conduct this type of research in your organization. You learned how to use control groups and experimental groups to conduct experiments, isolate variables using regression analysis, and interpret the results of a regression analysis. You have the tools, now it's time to use them!

5.6 Absenteeism

Absenteeism is another area that organizations are keen to understand. On average, absenteeism costs approximately $26.4 billion every year in the United States (Steers and Rhodes, 1978). This figure should be enough to convince you that absenteeism is worth studying, not to mention the headaches of trying to staff appropriately and deal with the "no-shows" right before shift starts. The following example is a real situation I ran across, when working with a pharmaceutical manufacturing plant, on ways to prevent unwanted absenteeism. The data in the chart below represents the average absenteeism rate by day for first shift production workers, at this plant, over a one-month period.

Figure 5.2

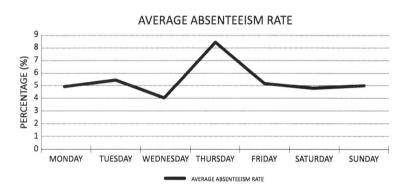

AVERAGE ABSENTEEISM RATE

Discussion Question:

Why do you think absenteeism spikes on Thursday?

Solution to the above question can be downloaded from the
Online Resources section of this book on **www.vibrantpublishers.com**

5.7 Metrics

We've already reviewed several metrics along the way, both in this chapter and others. Many metrics for the nonexempt workforce will depend on that workforce. For example, you would have different metrics for production workers in a plant than you would have for a bank teller or sanitation worker. It is up to each organization to determine the appropriate metrics for their given workforce; however, some common metrics might include the following:

- Employee engagement

- Absenteeism

- Turnover

- Labor costs

- Safety incidents

- Benefits usage

Like other discussions we have had on metrics, the intent of these measures is to help the organization monitor various points within the employment relationship that benefit both the organization and the employee. Although many metrics are common and used across organizations, it is incumbent on HR employees (sometimes with the help of analytics teams) to determine the right metrics and how to measure the appropriate information in each situation.

Chapter Summary

◆ The nonexempt workforce is one of the greatest "untapped" sources of data for many organizations and understand how to use those data can help the organization and its employees be more productive and engaged.

◆ The hourly hiring process is an area that can be analyzed using advanced techniques.

◆ Utility analysis can be used to quantify the effectiveness of various hiring methods.

◆ Using analytics in the collective bargaining process can be beneficial to both sides and create a "win/win" scenario.

◆ Productivity analysis is an important area for many organizations and can be quantified using analytical techniques.

CASE STUDY:
ManuCo Hourly Hiring Utility Analysis

The following case study will give you a chance to practice conducting a utility analysis. Reference the "Utility Analysis" section above for a refresher and example of how to complete the case.

Overview

Understanding the value of a selection methodology, especially for high turnover jobs that are sometimes found in the hourly workforce is critical. Because so many employees go through the hourly hiring process, we need to know how the process is being translated into results for the organization. This case follows Grace, the head of analytics at ManuCo as she navigates the hourly hiring process and potentially finds several areas for improvement.

Background

As Grace sat outside of the conference room waiting for her turn to be called into the executive committee meeting, she reviewed her slides and recommendations with a bit of nervousness. Grace was confident that she had done the proper analysis, and that she had good data. However, the recommendation was going to be a big change for ManuCo, and she wasn't sure how the executive committee would react. She sat pensively and remembered back to when she was first hired three years ago as the manager of people analytics at ManuCo. At that point in time, she was asked to help design and develop an analytics department from the ground up. Although she felt she had made some progress with the function, she knew that the recommendations she was about to make would be the most impactful of her career thus far.

Grace was hired by her boss, Martin, the VP of HR. Martin had been at ManuCo for well over 20 years and was very invested in how business was done within the organization. He had spent his career in HR, mostly supporting the manufacturing function in various plants around the world, and had climbed the corporate ladder to his current position as the head of HR for ManuCo, a 50,000 employee company that was one of the biggest manufacturing companies in the region. The organization was well known as a good place to work, especially for hourly positions. When an hourly position would open, there were often several hundred applicants. And because the supply of talent was so high, the recruiting team would have to screen candidates to find the right person.

Grace was hired by Martin to start the people analytics function and bring a new focus on evidence-based human resources and employee relations to ManuCo. At the time she was hired, she recalled that ManuCo had set out to implement a new hourly hiring strategy to achieve three objectives. Those objectives were the following:

1. Reduce net operating costs through stronger job performance as measured by increased productivity and quality, reduced turnover and absenteeism, and fewer on-the-job injuries.

2. Mitigate legal risk.

3. Reshape and realign the hourly workforce with continuous improvement efforts.

Although Grace was not directly involved with this project at the time, it was a huge undertaking that everyone in HR knew about, and it was all the buzz around the office.

Outside Help

In order to achieve these objectives and satisfy a very tight timeframe for hiring, Martin planned to hire an expert consulting firm to design, implement, and administer ongoing hiring assessments for the hourly workforce. In order to find this consulting firm, ManuCo went through a very detailed request for proposal process; however, timelines were tight and the process was rushed. The winning firm was hired based on previous reputation and reported industry expertise. This consulting firm had worked with many of the big players in the same industry as ManuCo, and told the steering committee that their recommended hiring process for hourly employees was, by all industry standards, a best practice. This consulting firm also informed ManuCo that its current hiring process may be out of line with best practice, based on their expert opinion.

The assessment methodology the consulting firm proposed was comprised of two parts (see Figure 5.1). The first part was a hands-on simulation. During this simulation, candidates were asked to screw in nuts and bolts in various stations, and use their hands to perform job tasks similar to what would be done if they were hired. Throughout the simulation, candidates were also engaged in safety-related activities as best as they could, without being taken onto the actual production floor. This piece of the selection assessment was scored and counted 2.5x towards an individual's total score. The second part of the assessment was a personality test completed on a computer. The personality tests took approximately 90 minutes to complete and were comprised of approximately 200 questions. Those questions were geared towards assessing the "Big Five" personality traits including: conscientiousness, openness to new experiences, neuroticism, extroversion, and agreeableness. Each personality trait was broken down into several different questions that were scored and summed. The personality portion of the assessment was weighted 1x towards an individual's total score.

In order to implement this new assessment methodology, ManuCo needed to make some changes within its plants and other administrative buildings. First, they needed to allocate space for an assessment center in each plant location. The space needed for the hands-on simulation and computer personality tests required approximately 1300 ft² in total. The assessment centers were then placed in areas where there were unique hiring needs, or where there were several plants within driving distance. In total, ManuCo had to set up five of these assessment centers. In addition to the cost of setting up the centers, the ongoing administration costs that were paid to the consulting firm totaled $3.5 million each year. This administration fee was paid to the vendor to administer the personality tests, score them, proctor the hands-on simulation, and generate individual reports with hiring recommendations. The scheduling of the assessments was done by ManuCo, and each assessment center had their own full-time resource to schedule assessments.

Before the assessment centers were set up in each location, the consulting firm worked with ManuCo to determine a group of experts who would rate the importance of various competencies that would be tested in the assessment. They surveyed over 500 front-line supervisors to better understand the organization and the competencies which ManuCo was looking for in their hourly employees. The results of the survey, including the mean importance score and standard deviation for each competency, are included in Table 5.3.

Table 5.3

Competency	Importance Rating	
	Mean	SD
Safety Awareness	2.49	0.80
Applied Learning	4.08	0.75
Initiating Action	4.00	0.88
Quality Orientation	1.09	0.73
Work Standards	3.22	0.79
Communication	3.96	1.02
Adaptability	4.11	0.76
Problem Solving/Decision Making	3.99	0.94
Energy	3.96	0.80
Contributing to Team Success	4.19	0.83
Continuous Improvement	1.49	0.88

Once it was determined which competencies were important, the consulting firm then created an algorithm to calculate individual weighted scores for the personality test and hands-on simulation. The personality test was weighted as one times (1x) the person's score, and the hands-on simulation was weighted at 2.5 times (2.5x) the person's score. In order to pass, a candidate must have scored above the 20th percentile on both the personality test and the hands-on simulation. Percentiles were calculated using the average scores from the consulting firm's book of business, which had given similar personality tests in the past. The total candidate score was also calculated as a sum of the personality test score and the hands-on test score. The total score had to be above the 60th percentile.

Figure 5.3   **Assessment Methodology**

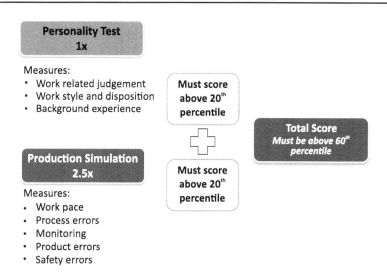

ManuCo thought that because the consulting firm had worked in their industry and had several competitors as clients, the algorithm would work just fine in their environment. No modifications were made to the weightings of either part of the assessment. Grace recalled hearing that when the new system was implemented, there was some confusion about the results of the survey and the stated goals of the organization.

Several months later Grace was grabbing a cup of coffee in the break room and overheard some colleagues talking about the hiring that was going on at the plants. She did not want to interrupt and ask further questions, but it was clear that they were not that pleased with some of the most recent hires. Grace heard her colleague Frank say, "You know, these new hourly folks just don't get it." Another colleague said, "I have seen the highest turnover in my plant from as far back as I can remember." Grace got her cup of coffee, took mental notes of the comments, and went about her day.

Current State Analysis

About a year later Grace was leading a line supervisor focus group project, to assess the new performance management system that had just been put in place. But somehow, the conversation turned to hiring. Again, it was clear that the supervisors were not pleased with the quality of hires in the most recent group of hourly employees. One supervisor said, "We still have not adapted the continuous improvement mindset. Isn't that project over by now?" Another comment by a supervisor was, "We had another quality issue at two of our plants that will likely result in recall." Even more, another supervisor said, "I really don't trust that these new hires will ever really care about doing a good job."

When Grace finished with the focus group, she headed to her next meeting which happened to be with Mary, the plant manager. Although she was there to talk about the new performance system, Grace wanted to first get Mary's reaction to the feedback she had heard in the focus group. To her dismay, Grace heard from the plant manager that, "I don't know the last time that we had a decent hire. That's not fair, we have some, but it just seems like we've hit a rough patch with our hiring of hourly employees." As Grace was driving home from yet another plant visit, she received a call on her cell phone that she would never forget. It was Martin and he was clearly upset. After calming him down and assuring him that she could help, he explained the situation to her. Apparently, in addition to the safety issues that she had heard about in her focus group several months earlier, there had been other recalls due to quality issues in other plants. The head of manufacturing had heard enough. Martin told Grace that he needed her to do an analysis of the current program so that he could have an evidenced-based way to decide about the future of ManuCo hiring its hourly employees.

Because Grace knew that she was on a tight timeframe, she decided to conduct a concurrent validation study for the hiring process. This study consisted of gathering three sets of data from current ManuCo employees. The first two sets of data would be gathered from hourly production employees. She would ask them to take time from their jobs to complete both the personality test and the hands-on simulation. The third set of data she needed would be from the supervisors of these hourly employees. She would ask the supervisors to rate each of the hourly employees on their performance. Grace defined performance in a few different ways: she looked at the number of safety incidents for each employee, the number of unexplained absences for each employee, the employee's ability to do the job as judged by the supervisor, and the speed at which the employee could do his or her job. Each supervisor was asked to rate their direct reports, and then provide a measure of how well they felt they could rate those employees. Grace used this data to filter out any employee who may not be familiar to that particular supervisor.

Grace was able to gather data from over a thousand hourly employees and their supervisors. She then filtered the data and removed any employee who either did not complete both parts of the assessment, or whose supervisor did not feel that he or she could make an accurate assessment. The resulting sample of employees was just over 750.

After doing some preliminary descriptive statistics on her data, Grace looked at the relationship between scores on the current assessment and those measures of performance. Based on her analysis, she found that according to the US Department of labor standards, the personality test was useful "depending on the circumstances," the production or hands-on simulation was "less likely to be useful," and the overall score was "less likely to be useful." (Department of Labor guidelines and the results of her study are pictured in Table 5.4.)

Table 5.4

Assessment	Initial Scoring* (Overall Performance Composite)	Dept. of Labor Guideline
Personality Test	.19	Depends on circumstances
Production Simulation	.09	Less likely to be useful
Total Score	.10	Less likely to be useful

Figure 5.4   Relationship Between Job Performance and Total Score

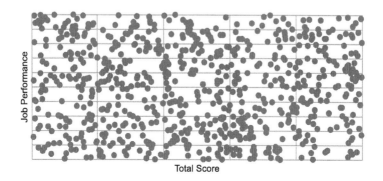

Options

Based on her experience and her academic background, Grace knew that showing these results would simply not be good enough. In order to "sell" her recommendations to the steering committee, she would have to conduct a utility analysis. She also needed to satisfy Martin's request to base her recommendations on empirical data. Grace explored four options for how to proceed.

The first option was maintaining the status quo. ManuCo would keep their current vendor and have a discussion with the client manager regarding a better understanding of the assessments. They might be able to tweak the current assessments to better suit their needs. Although the ManuCo organization was not currently thrilled with that vendor, it would be the fastest way to a solution that may improve the hourly hiring process.

The second option was to expand the scope of a different vendor. As Grace was conducting her analysis and doing some internal research, she learned of another vendor operating in a similar capacity in a different region. It was also contracted to conduct hiring assessments for hourly employees. Unlike ManuCo's first vendor, this other vendor had a great reputation, and although there hadn't been a concurrent validation study completed, anecdotal feedback was positive about the people who were hired under this assessment process.

The third option was for Grace to recommend that ManuCo bring the hands-on simulation in-house and administer the assessment themselves. This would clearly take time to set up, and they may have to hire new employees to administer the new assessment.

The fourth and final option was to design an in-house, hands-on simulation including a structured interview. Grace got the idea of the structured interview through her work during the research phase of this project. As she was interviewing supervisors and HR managers in the various plants, she heard several times they felt that they could select employees who would be better fit for the job if they could just sit down with them and conduct an interview. Although somewhat unconventional for hourly employees, Grace wanted to make sure that she did her due diligence and explored all the options.

In order to conduct her utility analysis, Grace calculated the expected monetary gain for each of the options. (Here analysis inputs are shown in Table 5.5.)

Table 5.5

Utility Analysis Factor	Vendor 1 (Current Test)	Vendor 2 (Personality Assessment Only)	In-house Production Simulation	In-house Production Simulation + Behavioral-based, Highly Structured Interview
Number of Hires (Ns)	500	500	500	500
Test Validity (r)	0.1	0.2	0.3	0.5
Standard Dev. of Test Performance* (SD)	$20,000	$20,000	$20,000	$20,000
Average Test Score of Those Selected (Z)	0.5	0.9	1.0	1.1
Number of People Assessed (Nr)	700	700	700	700
Cost of Assessment (C)	$250	$200	$50	$100

*Using 40% rule

Expected monetary gain = Ns * r * SD * Z – (Nr * C)

As she sat outside the meeting room, Grace was confident that she would make the right recommendation. She had done her homework, talked to several different stakeholders throughout the research phase, and did a thorough analysis of the four options. Upon reviewing those options, she had a clear recommendation to the committee and was excited, and a little nervous, to present her findings to some of the senior-most leaders within the organization. As the door to the meeting room opened, Grace took a deep breath, got up from her chair, and walked in.

Case Assignment

1. Comment on the approach that ManuCo took to design the hourly hiring process. What would you have recommended that they do differently?

2. What discrepancies do you see between the competency ratings in Table 5.3 and the stated hiring strategy?

3. What issues do you see with the weightings of each of the two parts of the assessment?

4. Comment on the relationship between job performance and total score as depicted in figure 5.4.

5. Calculate the expected monetary gain for each of the four options outlined in the case, and then make a recommendation of what ManuCo should do going forward.

Quiz 5

1. Analytics should not be used with the non-exempt workforce.

   a. True

   b. False

2. Which one of these is not a reason to use analytics with the exempt workforce?

   a. Productivity is often easier to measure

   b. Sample sizes tend to be bigger, allowing for easier experimentation

   c. Performance is often easier to measure

   d. There tends to be a better business case

3. What is a utility analysis?

   a. Something that power companies perform

   b. A detailed analysis of the usefulness of the HR function

   c. An analysis that quantifies, in monetary terms, the potential payoff of one assessment tool over another

   d. A way to select hourly employees

4. **When conducting a utility analysis, the z score does what?**

   a. Serves as an indication of the quality of the recruiting program

   b. Tells you who to hire

   c. Tells you how valid your assessment is

   d. Indicates the quality of your recruiters

5. **Based on the example in the collective bargaining section of this chapter, what should management do?**

   a. Give up

   b. Go back to the table and suggest technical training for everyone

   c. Hold strong and take a strike

   d. Push the latest and greatest soft skills training on the workforce

6. **What is the golden question in the minds of many executives?**

   a. Should I bring an umbrella today?

   b. How do I increase lunch breaks for my employees?

   c. What makes our workers more productive?

   d. How do I make the perfect scrambled egg?

7. What is the answer to why absenteeism spiked in the example in this chapter?

    a. People didn't like what was served for lunch on Thursday

    b. Commute times were worse on Thursdays

    c. There was a train that passed through town every Thursday before shift start

    d. There was a bowling league on Wednesday nights

8. What project would be appropriate to do with the hourly workforce?

    a. A study on absenteeism

    b. A project to predict turnover

    c. Bargaining analytics

    d. All of the above

Solutions to the above questions can be downloaded from the **Online Resources** *section of this book on* **www.vibrantpublishers.com**

Chapter **6**

Getting Started

The following section is a reflection on the previous chapters and ties the content from each of those chapters (plus turnover and diversity) to the self-assessment that you completed in Chapter 1. Each content area is then broken down into the Four Roles of HR Analytics to provide you a place to start, based on the role that you selected. This chapter builds on one of the central tenants of this book - you need to meet the organization and its leaders "where they are." If your organization is not ready for predictive analytics, do not try to deliver predictive analytics. If your organization is ready for benchmarks and dashboards, deliver those first and use those "quick wins" to build upon.

Key learning objectives include the following:

- Further understanding of the Capability / Readiness Matrix

- Understanding of how to apply the role of the reader to each of the topics covered in this book

- How to get started on an analytics project in each of the topic areas covered earlier in this book, depending on where the reader falls on the Capability / Readiness Matrix

- Applying the knowledge gained by completing the case study at the end of the chapter

6.1 Capability / Readiness Matrix

The Capability / Readiness Matrix quiz and matrix are below for your reference.

Figure 6.1

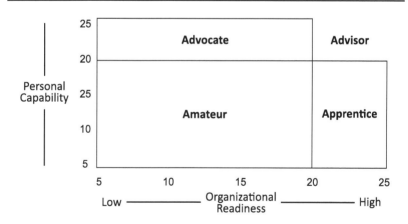

Personal Ability	I am comfortable conducting applied research in an organizational setting.	
	I know how to apply statistics to solve an organizational need.	
	I can manipulate data in a spreadsheet or data analysis tool (e.g. MS Excel, Google Sheets, SPSS, etc.).	
	I am comfortable using data to communicate my ideas.	
	I can condense a large amount of qualitative data (e.g., interview notes) into meaningful trends or themes.	
	Personal Ability Total	
Organizational Readiness	My organization uses data to make decisions on a regular basis.	
	Leaders within my organization are comfortable interpreting data from charts.	
	My organization has a formal "business analytics" function.	
	My organization looks to improve the way things are done.	
	My organization has formal training for employees to learn about analytics.	
	Organizational Readiness Total	
Your Role:		

6.2 Recruiting

As mentioned in Chapter 2, recruiting is one of the areas in HR that can benefit the most from using analytics. Because the typical recruiting process is monitored and measured in such granular detail, we can collect and utilize those data from an analytics perspective. The unfortunate tale is that many organizations don't! Regardless of what quadrant you and your organization fall into, there is always work to be done with recruiting data. Let's look at potential areas of focus based on the role that you play.

6.2.1 Amateur

When in the role of an amateur as it relates to the recruiting process, it is most important to get your hands on the recruiting data that your organization collects. Understanding the recruiting process through data will help you set the foundation for more advanced analysis later. Understanding what each of the different phases in the recruiting process means, how the data is collected, and what you could potentially do with it is the key. A good place to start if you are in the amateur quadrant is to work with your HRIT group (or person) and recruiting partners to better understand the data that you may have.

Once you understand the data that you have access to, you can start to use those data for trend and demographic analysis. Using basic analytic techniques such as counts and averages, you can start to tell a story with your recruiting data. One of the most critical and most used reports that you may start to generate is called a funnel report. A funnel report represents the number of candidates within each step of the recruiting process from "applicant" all the way to "hire." The funnel report is a visual way to depict how many individuals are in each stage of the process. This can give you a good sense of where people are failing to progress in the recruiting process. For example, looking at a job, do candidates fall out at the resume screening step? If so, you may want to revisit your sourcing strategy.

Another place to start in the amateur quadrant is to look at various metrics such as "time to fill." Defining these metrics for your organization can be a task in and of itself, however, is well worth the effort. Not only will you become more knowledgeable about the recruiting process and how to measure it, but your efforts will also help to train the organization on how to do the same. For example, time to fill is a great metric to look at because it leads to many more questions. One of these questions could be, "If we have a time to fill that is longer than desired, where is the process being held up?" You can then look at the number of days spent in each step of the "funnel" to help isolate where the bottlenecks exist. For example, if you realize that your time to fill is 100 days and resumes are being hung up in the hiring manager review stage, you can speak with your hiring managers or put in process improvements such as automatic notifications if those resumes are not passed along quickly.

As mentioned in chapter 1 the amateur quadrant is all about learning. Learning for you and learning for the organization. One way to do this is through basic understanding of the information that you are collecting and metrics that highlight process inefficiencies.

6.2.2 Advocate

If you fall in the advocate role as it relates to recruiting, your job is to continue to educate the organization. You can do this through several different ways. Building on an understanding of the current data that you collect and what it means, you can now take the next step in using your own personal capability to help educate the organization. Projects like funnel analysis by gender is a good place to start. This type of analysis can open the door for broader conversation about gender diversity, sourcing, and inherent bias. Depending on the level of organizational readiness within the advocate quadrant, you may be able to use your skills to look at performance of employees hired from various sources, and start looking into your hiring methodologies such as assessments (i.e., validity and reliability) to determine if you have the right processes in place.

Another place to start if you are an advocate is to look at how employees move into, around, and out of your organization. Depicting the flows of labor within and out of the organization is generally a good place to start to educate the organization and open the door for broader policy discussions. Remember, in the advocate quadrant, it is your responsibility to use your skills and capability to educate the organization and bring them further along in the analytics journey.

6.2.3 Apprentice

The important part about being an apprentice is that you are learning from the rest of the organization. In order to do this under the guise of recruiting, your best first step could be to speak with people who have recently been recruited to the organization. Collecting qualitative data through focus groups, interviews, and other means will help you learn more about the recruiting function and how it is performing. Don't forget to use the qualitative data analysis and coding exercises found earlier in this book.

In terms of learning technical skills from the organization, there are several avenues that you could take. The first is to find a mentor. Finding a mentor or someone who is very technically capable is a great way to start "dipping your toe" further into the analytics pool. Your objectives for the mentorship should be things like learning technical skills, understanding how to ask more technical questions, and how to present data to a technical audience. A mentor should be able to help you through each of those objectives within a reasonable timeframe.

The second avenue to gain better technical skills is to volunteer for a project that is outside of your comfort zone. Make sure that you are pairing up with a project team or leader who has something to do with the recruiting function. If your organization outsources the screening and data analysis part of the recruiting process, see if you can team up with your recruiting vendor to learn from them. If not, see if you can find additional work to learn more technical skills as it relates to the recruiting function.

6.2.4 Advisor

Being an advisor for the recruiting function as relates to analytics can open doors and help the organization uncover very powerful insights. When serving as an advisor the first step should be to collect qualitative data from various stakeholders, codify the data, and use those data to help you scope your first project.

An example of a project the you could take on would be to conduct a regression analysis using candidate source against performance outcomes while controlling for other variables. This will help the organization better understand where they're getting their best candidates and hires.

Another potential project would be to look at the differences in demographics between hiring managers and successful employees. For example, "Do younger hiring managers tend to hire younger and more diverse employees?" Or, "Do women tend to hire more women?" Again, using statistics and advanced analytics you should be able to isolate the impact of certain demographics on outcome variables.

As mentioned above, the recruiting function is full of potential areas for analytics. The key to the recruiting function is to ensure that your data is sound and that you are collecting the right types of data. As with any other function or analytics project you want to ensure that you know how the data are being used and what they mean. Once you have a better understanding of the data you will then be able to embark on your journey depending on the role in which you are currently serving.

6.3 Training impact

6.3.1 Amateur

When acting in the role of an amateur and trying to evaluate training impact, you should start with the front-end of the training needs analysis process to ensure that your training is grounded in organizational needs. See the "Training, Development, and

Careers" section of this book for information on how to conduct a needs analysis.

Once you have validated that your training is grounded in a thorough needs analysis, you can then start to measure its effectiveness. The first place to start would be with "happy sheets." Happy sheets ask participants about their opinions of the course. Statements might include things like, "My instructor was knowledgeable about topic," "The material was presented in an informational way," "The pre-work was appropriate," "I found this training beneficial," "I would recommend this training to my colleagues," etc. Starting with happy sheets will give you a good sense of how your audience feels about the training.

The next piece of information that you could gather is the knowledge gained from the training. In order to do this, you will need to ask participants to take a quiz before the training, then conduct the training, and have them take the same quiz after. This is level II in Kirkpatrick's model of training evaluation. You can then look at the difference between scores before the training and after the training to determine if the training has made a difference. At this point, you do not need to know any kind of statistical method or test, only if there is a difference in scores. This can help you start to build the business case for that course or curriculum. Keep in mind that this is not as statistically sound as conducting a more advanced type of analysis; however, in this role, your organization is likely not yet ready for anything more advanced.

6.3.2 Advocate

When acting in an advocate role, it is important to help the organization understand which training makes a difference and which training does not. In order to do this, you may be able to draw upon some of the lessons learned above in the amateur role and take them to the next level.

One place to start would be the increase of knowledge after taking the training course. Whereas in the amateur role, you are just looking to see if there is a difference in scores between the pretest and posttest, in the advocate role, we can now apply statistical methods such as t-tests to those data. Not only will we be able to say if there is a difference or not, but we will be able to say if that difference is statistically significant.

Another place for an advocate to start would be in the perception of behavior change after a training class. This will require the design of a survey or another method of observation that is sent to or utilized by managers of the employees who took the training. Because survey design and development take more skill and the ability to ensure reliability and validity, this task falls into the advocate bucket. Based on this analysis, you will be able to determine if employees have changed their behaviors based on the training. This is Kirkpatrick's level III analysis.

6.3.3 Apprentice

In the apprentice role, you can learn a lot from the organization. You can start with anecdotal feedback about various training classes which can be gathered through one on one interviews or focus groups. This will give you a sense of which training courses have the perception of working versus not. Using this anecdotal feedback, you can work with a partner to learn how to create happy sheets and manager surveys. You can then use the methods described in the advocate role to measure training effectiveness.

6.3.4 Advisor

When playing an advisor role, it is critical that you help the organization understand the value of the training courses that are being conducted. Your analyses should advance beyond simple statistical analysis such as t-tests and move more into predictive analytics and business impact.

Business impact can be measured through several different outcome variables. The first variable, and possibly the most intuitive variable, would be some measure of performance. For example, if you have a course on value selling that all salespeople need to take, you could do an analysis on whether that course results in higher sales. Using advanced techniques such as regression and structural equation modeling, you can incorporate other variables and control for extraneous information. Presenting this information to various stakeholders can help the organization realize the value of its training (or not) and ensure the right allocation of resources.

6.4 Total Rewards - Pay Equity

In the area of total rewards, one of the first places that an HR practitioner might want to start is with pay equity. Pay equity is a topic that is of growing importance and is an area where HR analytics can help drive further discussion into the organization. It is important to note that, before you embark on a pay equity study, you should first consult with your legal council as some of the findings of your analysis could get a bit tricky to communicate and understand. Let's look at where you could start, based on the results of your assessment above.

6.4.1 Amateur

At the amateur level, it is critically important to understand if the organization believes that it has a pay equity issue or not. Sometimes, you can better understand the perception of a pay equity issue by simply speaking with others. At the amateur level you should be able to conduct focus groups or interviews to better understand the perceptions of the employees within the organization. When it comes to pay equity, these perceptions can become reality which is why it is so important to address pay equity on a regular basis.

Once you have determined the organizational perspective on pay equity, you can then start to analyze some simple demographic information. For example, does the organization pay for performance? Do men make more than women in the same job? Are you paying for tenure? The answers to these questions can sometimes be answered with simple demographic cuts of data. This is where you should start in order to increase your knowledge as well as that of the organization.

6.4.2 Advocate

In the advocate role, is important to help the organization understand if and where pay inequities exist. If the organization is not ready for a full-blown pay equity analysis, you should not try to force the issue. Because pay equity is one of the most debated issues within organizations, starting down this path may not help to advance your analytics cause. Starting with basic statistics and demographic information may allow various stakeholders to get on board before attempting and more advanced type of analysis.

6.4.3 Apprentice

As with an apprentice in a machine shop or forging facility, not knowing what you are doing when it comes to pay equity analysis can cause more harm than good. In the apprentice role, it is critical that you learn from those around you. In this case, I would suggest that you learn from your legal partners and other internal and external experts about the right way to conduct a pay equity analysis. Equity analysis can be misinterpreted easily, and the wrong conclusions can be drawn if you do not know how to interpret the data. When performing in an apprentice role as it relates to pay equity, the most important part is to partner with a mentor who can help you to better understand the interpretation of pay equity analysis.

6.4.4 Advisor

There have been many steps taken to ensure pay equity within organizations. Although much work is been done, much more needs to be done. Understanding what is truly going on within a given organization is often more impactful than overall societal trends. The interventions that have been implemented at a societal level are often with good intentions, however, can be misleading. Even the positive impact that some of these interventions have had on society may not impact individual employees. The question for an advisor is, "How can we impact pay equity for an individual organization or even a business unit within an organization?" Descriptive statistics are generally not enough. In this case, we must rely on our good friend, the regression analysis.

Running descriptive statistics such as the average pay for men versus women is a good start, but they can be deceptive. Before you recommend massive increases for individuals in a demographic group, you need to first understand the dynamics of the organization and its employees. Using regression analysis, we can control for things like geography, performance (which could also be biased, so we need to be careful), tenure, career level, types of jobs, etc. This will help you better understand what dynamics are occurring within your organization. For example, look at Figure 6.2. We can see that the gender pay gap in this example is not as straightforward as one might think.

Figure 6.2   **Gender Pay Gap Explained**

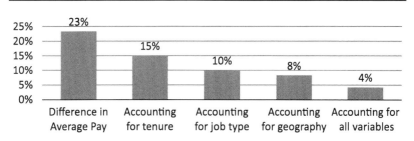

If we are to just look at the difference in average pay for men and women, we might argue that we should give every woman in this company a pay raise of 23%. Although some of the women in the sample may deserve that magnitude of increase, will be overpaying many others. We can also see that, as we take certain other characteristics into account, the pay gap decreases. Finally, if we include all variables in a regression model, we can see that the gap decreases to 4%. Although that is still a pay gap that should be addressed, is much less than what we thought in the beginning. The work after modeling includes looking at the pay for individual employees to determine if and how much their pay should be increased. In the advisor role, it is important to remember that the answer might not be what is directly in front of you, but to let the analysis guide the discussion and decisions being made.

6.5 Employee Turnover

Employee turnover is a metric that is often talked about in organizations and the popular press alike. The loss of a high performing employee or newly hired employee can not only be detrimental to the organization but to the teams of employees who are "left behind." Unwanted turnover is an issue that many organizations struggle with and is one that can cost up to 4-5 times an employee's annual salary.

Not only can analytics functions and HR practitioners deliver value quickly through turnover analysis, but the data needed for turnover analysis is usually housed within HR data systems. This means that that data is reasonably easy to obtain compared to something like sales performance data that might be housed in another system that is maintained within the sales function. Using data that reside within the HR system(s) requires much less "selling" to stakeholders outside of the function. This allows for the analysis to start much quicker and for recommendations to come faster as well.

6.5.1 Amateur

Because turnover is a phenomenon that impacts so many different parts of the organization, at the amateur level you can really start to educate yourself and the organization about the importance of turnover and where you can make the biggest impact.

One of the first things you can do is to define turnover metrics. Defining metrics like "unwanted turnover" versus turnover that the organization plans for can be critically important. Turnover of certain demographic groups can also be impactful to the organization. Starting with the definition of important turnover metrics is a great place for an amateur to start.

Another way to demonstrate impact and value is to collect information to start calculating the cost of turnover. The cost of turnover can be a tricky metric to calculate, due to many of the costs being "soft costs." These costs are often hard to quantify and include things like "loss of productivity" and "team member morale."

6.5.2 Advocate

When acting as an advocate, you can start to help the organization understand the cost of turnover. A simple internet search can produce many different definitions to help you better understand what should go into the cost of turnover. Quantifying things like "lost productivity," "onboarding cost," "exit survey administration," "team member productivity, loss or burnout," etc. can all be areas to use your advanced analytic skills and educate the organization.

Once you've quantified the cost of turnover, you can start to help the organization better understand why this phenomenon is such an important metric to measure and monitor. Creating dashboards and easy ways to look at turnover data can be another impactful place to start for an advocate.

6.5.3 Apprentice

If you fall into the apprentice category, there are lots of ways that you can learn from the organization. Not only can you learn technical skills about how to conduct advanced turnover analytics, but you can also learn from employees who might be at high risk of turnover. Talking to these employees in various demographic groups can help you to better understand the dynamics within the organization and the experiences that each of these employees has within the organization. Turnover analytics does not have to be difficult or technically advanced, but it should be logically sound and informational for the organization.

6.5.4 Advisor

When it comes to turnover one of the most interesting analyses that an advisor can conduct is a logistic regression based on employment outcomes. This means that you would conduct a regression with the binary outcome of "if the employee is still with the organization or not." Incorporating variables such as demographics, labor market rates, educational qualifications, promotional rates, team dynamics, manager dynamics, etc. are all great things to include however, need to be based in prior research. Conducting prior research on turnover should include academic literature as well as internal organizational anecdotes. The combination of these two sources of data should give you a good place to start and think about the variables to include in the analysis.

The results of this analysis should produce questions and recommendations for policy changes aimed at decreasing unwanted turnover. These conversations need to be had at high levels of the organization because recommendations could fundamentally change how the organization operates.

Some organizations take turnover modeling to the next level. Based on the results of your regression modeling, you could now put together an algorithm that produces probabilities of leaving for individuals within an organization. Not all organizations (and quite frankly not all analytics professionals) are comfortable taking this analysis to this level of detail, making it important that you consult with your legal team before embarking. Using an algorithm to predict who may or may not leave could result in things like stay interviews for your top performers who might leave, however leaders and HR managers need to be armed with information and understanding on how this algorithm works, what it means, and what it doesn't mean. Again, I want to stress the importance of consulting with legal counsel before embarking on this type of analysis.

6.6 A Note About Inclusion and Diversity Analysis

Inclusion and diversity are some of the most pressing issues facing organizations (and society) right now. Many organizations struggle with finding the right way to speak about inclusion and diversity, let alone make meaningful strides in the right direction. Although we will not dive too deep into this topic in this book out of the inability to get into enough detail while covering all relevant topics, analytics can be a great place to start. Organizations that have a difficult time starting the conversation can rely on analytics to lead the way.

The other reason why I will not focus on inclusion and diversity analysis is because there is not one "inclusion and diversity" analysis. All processes and policies within an organization should be looked at through an I&D lens. This means including variables such as gender, ethnicity, age, etc. into each analysis that you do. Recruiting should be scrutinized to include diverse group analysis. Training class outcomes should be looked at through an I&D lens (e.g., Do younger people learn more than their older counterparts? If so, what can we do about it?). Pay equity should be reviewed on a regular basis. Promotions and salary increases should be analyzed and looked at through an I&D lens, etc.

I want to be clear on this point I am not omitting specific I&D analyses because they lack importance, I am omitting them because they are so important that they should be included in every other type of analysis that you do, in whatever form that takes and in whatever role you are serving.

Chapter Summary

◆ There are several areas where you can get started,
based on your position in the Capability / Readiness
Matrix.

◆ The key to starting in analytics is to tailor your starting
point to the role that you currently play.

◆ Inclusion and diversity analysis should be included in
every analysis that you do. It is a critical lens through
which all data should be viewed.

CASE STUDY:
The Four Roles of HR Analytics

Maria

Although Maria was not new to the function of HR, she was new to analytics. She could do basic analysis in Microsoft Excel and was excited to learn more. She had taken several analytics classes part of her MBA program and knew how to conduct research and manage a project within an organization. She was certain that she could do more with data if she could just have a situation where she could apply her knowledge. She had given several presentations with data in them; however, she had received feedback from her boss that she used too many charts and graphs. She had also been encouraged to learn how to better tell a story with data. She was a bit confused on how to best select the right statistical test to solve a problem; however, she knew basics like how to calculate means and t-tests. She knew that, with a bit of help, she would be able to find a way to apply what she knew to the organization and make an impact.

EngineerCo.

Engineer Co. was an engineering firm. The culture was one that could be described as friendly, but data driven. Oftentimes, business leaders would ask for even more data than what people were comfortable presenting because leaders were had an insatiable appetite for data. The business analytics function had created some classes for people to take that were supposed to help with analytical skills, but they didn't get great reviews and were reportedly not very good. There had been a few attempts to make the training better and more applicable for those who would use it every day; however, resources have been diverted for other things. Although EngineerCo. said that it was ready to embark on the HR analytics journey, questions about their true readiness abound.

Case Assignment

1. Rate Maria and EngineerCo on the Four Roles of Analytics Matrix. What score did you give to Maria's personal capability? What score did you give to EngineerCo?

Personal Ability	I am comfortable conducting applied research in an organizational setting.	
	I know how to apply statistics to solve an organizational need.	
	I can manipulate data in a spreadsheet or data analysis tool (e.g. MS Excel, Google Sheets, SPSS, etc.)	
	I am comfortable using data to communicate my ideas.	
	I can condense a large amount of qualitative data (e.g., interview notes) into meaningful trends or themes.	
	Personal Ability Total	
Organizational Readiness	My organization uses data to make decisions on a regular basis.	
	Leaders within my organization are comfortable interpreting data from charts.	
	My organization has a formal "business analytics" function.	
	My organization looks to improve the way things are done.	
	My organization has formal training for employees to learn about analytics.	
	Organizational Readiness Total	
Maria's Role:		

2. What role is Maria playing?

3. What could Maria do to learn more about analytics and how to tell a story with data?

4. What project should Maria tackle next?

Quiz 6

1. What role is in the upper right quadrant of the Capability / Readiness Matrix?

    a. Advocate

    b. Advisor

    c. Apprentice

    d. Amateur

2. What would be a good project for someone in the Advisor role in the recruiting function?

    a. Running demographic information about who has been hired

    b. Partnering with someone from an analytics function to better understanding the correlation between school graduated from and on the job performance for front line leaders

    c. Predicting performance on the job based on school attended and other factors, using multiple regression

    d. Using survey methods to better understand candidate views of the recruiting process

3. **What would be a good project for someone in the Apprentice role in the recruiting function?**

   a. Running demographic information about who has been hired

   b. Partnering with someone from an analytics function to better understanding the correlation between school graduated from and on the job performance for front line leaders

   c. Predicting performance on the job based on school attended and other factors, using multiple regression

   d. Using survey methods to better understand candidate views of the recruiting process

4. **What would be a good project for someone in the Amateur role in the training function?**

   a. Conducting a training needs analysis

   b. Partnering with the analytics function to understand the relationship between taking a training class and change in behavior on the job

   c. Predicting on the job performance based on several variables, including training taken

   d. Understanding the statistical differences in performance between those who took a training class and those who did not

5. **What would be a good project for someone in the Apprentice role in the training function?**

   a. Conducting a training needs analysis

   b. Partnering with the analytics function to understand the relationship between taking a training class and change in behavior on the job

   c. Predicting on the job performance based on several variables, including training taken

   d. Understanding the statistical differences in performance between those who took a training class and those who did not

6. **What would be a good project for someone in the Advocate role in the compensation function?**

   a. Understanding if the organization thinks that there is a pay equity issue through focus groups and interviews

   b. Running basic statistics and understanding the differences in pay between certain groups

   c. Partner with someone in the legal or employee relations function to conduct a pay analysis and learn more about how to properly conduct an equity analysis

   d. Predict pay based on compensable factors, among other external factors

7. **What would be a good project for someone in the Advisor role in the compensation function?**

    a. Understanding if the organization thinks that there is a pay equity issue through focus groups and interviews

    b. Running basic statistics and understanding the differences in pay between certain groups

    c. Partner with someone in the legal or employee relations function to conduct a pay analysis and learn more about how to properly conduct an equity analysis

    d. Predict pay based on compensable factors, among other external factors

8. **What would be a good project for someone in the Amateur role in the employee relations function?**

    a. Defining various turnover metrics like "quick quits" or "high performing turnover"

    b. Quantifying things like "exit survey administration" or "recruiting costs"

    c. Learning why employees might be leaving through interviews and focus groups

    d. Predicting turnover using internal factors, demographic factors and external factors

9. **What would be a good project for someone in the Advocate role in the employee relations function?**

   a. Defining various turnover metrics like "quick quits" or "high performing turnover"

   b. Quantifying things like "exit survey administration" or "recruiting costs"

   c. Learning why employees might be leaving through interviews and focus groups

   d. Predicting turnover using internal factors, demographic factors and external factors

10. **Which type of project should be approached from an Inclusion, Equity and Diversity perspective**

   a. Those that are sponsored by senior leadership

   b. Those that directly impact diverse employees

   c. Those that have legal implications

   d. Every. Single. One

Solutions to the above questions can be downloaded from the **Online Resources** *section of this book on* **www.vibrantpublishers.com**

This page is intentionally left blank

Chapter 7

In Closing

This chapter summarizes the rest of the book and gives the reader some tips to consider when embarking on the analytics journey. Because each of us are on our own journey as it relates to HR analytics, these tips are broadly applicable to everyone, regardless of how well you know about (or don't know about) HR analytics.

Key learning objectives include the following:

- Understanding of five things to consider regardless of where the reader might be on the analytics journey

- Knowledge of some closing thoughts and the author's thank you

Number 1: Know Your Data

We talked about a lot of things in this book. We talked about many different types of analyses and a lot of different things that you can do with data. As HR practitioners, we have access to so much data, and it is important that we understand what each of those data elements represent. I mentioned this in several places in the book; however, it is certainly worth mentioning again. Know your data. It is this fundamental understanding of the data that provides the background for your recommendations and action steps from your analysis. It is a bit cliché; however, the phrase, "garbage in, garbage out" truly does apply. Not only do you need to know if you have "bad" data but you need to know what each of your data elements means. Once you understand your data, then, and only then can you move forward with your analysis.

Number 2: Understand What You Can and Cannot Do (Yet!)

Understanding your own technical expertise is critical before embarking on an analysis. You can learn a lot from internet videos (and hopefully this book!) however analytics is not the place where you want to "fake it until you make it." Because you will have the eyes and ears of senior leaders looking at the outputs of your analysis and your recommendations, you could potentially have unintended consequences if your analyses are incorrect.

Earlier in this book, I tried to provide a simple framework for you to understand where you might fall in terms of your capability; however, please don't think that this is written in stone.

There are many ways that you can increase your capabilities, some of which are very simple to do. I hope you find this journey engaging and energizing and are excited to take your analytical capabilities to the next level!

Number 3: Know Your Organization

The second part of the capability/readiness matrix is all about your organization. I cannot stress enough how important it is to understand your organizational appetite to accept the kinds of analysis that you produce. Throughout my career I have worked with numerous organizations on every part of the organizational readiness scale. Learn from my mistakes. It is important to adapt your message and your methods to the organizational readiness because giving a 15-year-old the Ferrari is a great way for an accident to happen. In the case of HR analytics, your methodologies may not be accepted, and your recommendations may fall flat. The last thing we want to happen is that you create amazing analyses that sit on a shelf without any recommendations implemented because the organization was not ready.

Number 4: Think Differently

I hope that you learned about analytics in this book as it relates to the human resources function. I also hope that you learn how to ask the right types of questions and how to understand the world around us. Once you have a taste for analytics whether that be in a human resources function or any other discipline, your eyes begin to open around you to see all the data that surrounds you every day. I hope that you have a better understanding of what goes into some of the headlines that we see around the world and I hope that you continue to use analytics to make better decisions for yourself and those around you.

Number 5: "People Should Make People Decisions"

Prasad Setty (2014) of Google wisely said that one of the things he realized after joining Google and starting their People Analytics function was that, "people should make people decisions." In the most literal sense of that statement, I could not agree more. Using analytics and human resources data, we can help our leaders make decisions faster and better, but at the end of the day, people should still be making those decisions. The last thing that we want employees or managers to think is that we are going to take over HR processes with algorithms, machines or robots. As a discipline, HR is simply not there yet. Maybe someday in the future (don't ask me when) we will be more confident in the ability of artificial intelligence as it relates to the human resources function, however; today organizations are generally not ready for large scale implementation of AI in HR.

Some Closing Thoughts - My Hopes and a Thank You

I hope you enjoyed this book and learning more about the essentials of HR analytics.

I hope that my passion for this topic was able to come through these pages and I hope you enjoyed reading more about this important topic (If so, I hope you tell all your friends!).

I hope this book has changed the way you think about data and analytics, specifically to HR, but also the world around you.

I hope you use this book as a guide in your day to day life and I hope it helps you along your journey.

I hope that this book has piqued your interest in HR analytics, and I hope that you continue to push yourself to learn more.

Thank you. Thank you for taking the time to read this book as part of your learning journey. We are all on our own journey of continuous learning and I am honored to be a part of yours.

Chapter Summary

◆ There are five things that you should keep in mind when starting out or continuing your analytics journey – know your data, understand what you can and cannot do, know your organization, think differently and, "people should make people decisions."

◆ I hope you enjoyed the book and thank you for reading this book as part of your analytics journey.

Appendix: Getting Started with Excel – Video Tutorials

Basics of Microsoft Excel

The intent of this chapter is to ensure that everyone reading this book is on the same page in terms of technical abilities in Excel. We will use MS Excel throughout this book and a basic working knowledge of this program is important.

This chapter will feature several MS Excel modules which will highlight essential "how to" skills, such as saving a file, sorting data, formatting worksheets, writing basic formulas, inserting slicers, and manipulating pivot tables.

I hope this is a beneficial refresher for those who are familiar with Excel; and for those who are not, I hope that you learn a lot about this powerful tool!

The Excel Environment

For those who have never worked in Excel, the Excel environment can be a bit tricky to understand. For those who are familiar, this section will be a good refresher. This section covers how to open a dataset, a general tour of Excel, saving a file, headers and footers, and printing.

Intro and Opening Dataset

Starting with the very basic functionality of Excel, this video will present a high-level overview of Excel and teach you how to open a dataset.

Refer to the video **1_1 Intro and Opening Dataset.mp4** in **Online Resources** section of this book on **www.vibrantpublishers.com**

Excel Tour

This video reviews the overall look and feel of Excel and "tours" the screen, basic menu options, and how to operate in the Excel environment.

Refer to the video **1_2 Excel Tour.mp4** in **Online Resources** section of this book on **www.vibrantpublishers.com**

Saving and Header, Footer

This video will show you how to save a file in Excel as well as modify the document headers and footers for printing purposes.

 Refer to the video **1_3 Saving and Header Footer.mp4** in **Online Resources** section of this book on **www.vibrantpublishers.com**

Printing

This video will show you how to set your printing limits, select a printer and print the Excel document.

 Refer to the video **1_4 Printing.mp4** in **Online Resources** section of this book on **www.vibrantpublishers.com**

Basic Operations

In this section, we get more into the "meat" of Excel. Topics covered are: editing cells, selecting a range of cells, sorting and filtering.

Editing, Select Range, Copy

This video will cover several ways to edit the contents of a cell and how to select a range of cells within Excel.

 Refer to the video **2_1 Editing Select Range Copy Paste.mp4** in **Online Resources** section of this book on **www.vibrantpublishers.com**

Sorting and Filtering

This video will demonstrate how to sort data once it is loaded in an Excel spreadsheet as well as how to filter your data to manage the dataset.

 Refer to the video **2_2 Sorting and Filtering.mp4** in **Online Resources** section of this book on **www.vibrantpublishers.com**

Formatting

Getting even more advanced in terms of the look and feel of the spreadsheet and Excel environment, this section covers formatting and how to create drop-down menus.

Formatting

This video will introduce the formatting functionality in Excel and how to "pretty up" your spreadsheet. Afterall, no one wants to look at a boring spreadsheet!

Refer to the video **3_1 Formatting.mp4** in **Online Resources** section of this book on **www.vibrantpublishers.com**

Drop Downs

One of the most useful tools for managing your dataset, this video will introduce the drop down menu functionality within Excel.

Refer to the video **3_2 Drop Downs.mp4** in **Online Resources** section of this book on **www.vibrantpublishers.com**

Data Manipulation and Basic Formulas

Diving into actual capability of Excel, this section is all about how to manipulate your data once placed into an Excel spreadsheet. Also discussed are grouping areas of a spreadsheet, separating text to columns, and basic formulas.

Group and Text to Columns

Grouping your data is an important function when displaying data for others. Copying text into separate columns can be useful in many different scenarios. This video will demonstrate how to do both functions.

 Refer to the video **4_1 Group and Text to Columns.mp4** in **Online Resources** section of this book on **www.vibrantpublishers.com**

Basic Formulas

Creating, editing and using formulas is a very powerful functionality of Excel. This video will review some of the basic formulas that can be used in the Excel environment and how to use them.

 Refer to the video **4_2 Basic Formulas.mp4** in **Online Resources** section of this book on **www.vibrantpublishers.com**

Countif, vlookup, if statement

Wading into deeper water, this video will teach you how to use more advanced formulas like "count if" and "v lookup" to allow for ease of manipulating your data.

 Refer to the video **4_3 Countif vlookup if statement.mp4** in **Online Resources** section of this book on **www.vibrantpublishers.com**

Pivot Tables

Whether a newbie or a seasoned pro, one of the most valuable functionalities in Excel for an HR professional is the pivot table. This section is all about how to create and manipulate pivot tables to help with data analysis. Creation of graphs from a pivot table is also discussed.

 Refer to the video **5_1 Pivot Tables and Graphs.mp4** in **Online Resources** section of this book on **www.vibrantpublishers.com**

Charts and Graphs

Once you have analyzed your data, it is now time to visualize it. Excel can be a very intuitive and easy-to-use program for data visualization as well. This section is all about how to create and modify charts and graphs in Excel.

 Refer to the video **6_1 Charts and Graphs.mp4** in **Online Resources** section of this book on **www.vibrantpublishers.com**

Slicers

Getting more advanced in Excel, this section discusses the use and purpose of slicers. This functionality can be a very powerful tool when sharing data with others, or if needing to manipulate a dataset repeatedly. Slicers can also be used to create a user-friendly dashboard within the Excel environment. This section teaches you how to do exactly that.

 Refer to the video **7_1 Slicers.mp4** in **Online Resources** section of this book on **www.vibrantpublishers.com**

Putting It All Together

Once the data is analyzed, we need to put it into a story of some sort. This section walks through linked Excel files to PowerPoint, pasting charts, and telling a story with data.

PPT Outline and Linked Excel to PPT

This video will teach you how to outline your PowerPoint presentation and paste your Excel charts and graphs directly from your spreadsheet.

 Refer to the video **8_1 PPT Outline and Linked Excel to PPT. mp4** in **Online Resources** section of this book on **www.vibrantpublishers.com**

Pasting Charts and Data Story

This video will continue instruction about pasting charts into PowerPoint as well as how to tell a meaningful story with Excel data.

 Refer to the video **8_2 Pasting Charts and Data Story.mp4** in **Online Resources** section of this book on **www.vibrantpublishers.com**

Congratulations!

Whew! That was potentially a lot of information! My hope is that you were able to learn about the power of Microsoft Excel. Even if you were an avid MS Excel user before this chapter, I hope that you were able to take something away from the videos and practice.

References

Advisor. www.merriam-webster.com/dictionary/advisor?src=search-dict-hed.

Advocate. www.merriam-webster.com/dictionary/advocate?src=search-dict-hed.

Amateur. www.merriam-webster.com/dictionary/amateur?src=search-dict-hed.

Apprentice. www.merriam-webster.com/dictionary/apprentice?src=search-dict-hed.

Baron, J. N. (81). Kreps. D., 1999, Strategic Human Resources: Frameworks for General Managers.

Berger, L. A., & Berger, D. R. (Eds.). (2011). *The talent management handbook: Creating a sustainable competitive advantage by selecting, developing, and promoting the best people.* New York, NY: McGraw-Hill.

Bland, J. M., & Altman, D. G. (1994). Regression towards the mean. *BMJ: British Medical Journal, 308*(6942), 1499.

Brown, J. (2002). Training needs assessment: A must for developing an effective training program. *Public personnel management, 31*(4), 569-578.

Budd, J. W. (2010). Labor relations: Striking a balance. New York, NY: McGraw-Hill Irwin.

Eisenhardt, K. M. (1989). Agency theory: An assessment and review. Academy of management review, 14(1), 57-74.)

Gael, S. (1988). The job analysis handbook for business, industry, and government (Vol. 1). John Wiley & Sons.

Gale, E.A.M. (2004). The Hawthorne studies – a fable for our times? Quarterly Journal of Medicine, July, 97(7), 439-449.

Heneman, H. G., Judge, T., & Kammeyer-Mueller, J. D. (2003). Staffing organizations. Middleton, WI: Mendota House.

Hernán, M. A., Hernández-Díaz, S., & Robins, J. M. (2004). A structural approach to selection bias. *Epidemiology*, 615-625.

Jurs, S. G., & Glass, G. V. (1971). The effect of experimental mortality on the internal and external validity of the randomized comparative experiment. *The Journal of Experimental Education, 40*(1), 62-66.

Kassarjian, H. Content Analysis in Consumer Research, Journal of Consumer Research, Volume 4, Issue 1, June 1977, Pages 8–18, https://doi.org/10.1086/208674

Kirkpatrick, D., & Kirkpatrick, J. (2006). *Evaluating training programs: The four levels.* Berrett-Koehler Publishers.

Lawshe Jr, C. H. (1945). Studies in job evaluation: II. The adequacy of abbreviated point ratings for hourly-paid jobs in three industrial plants. Journal of Applied Psychology, 29(3), 177.

Levitt, S. D., & List, J. A. (2011). Was there really a Hawthorne effect at the Hawthorne plant? An analysis of the original illumination experiments. American Economic Journal: Applied Economics, 3(1), 224-38

Maheux, B., & Béland, F. (1987). Changes in students' sociopolitical attitudes during medical school: socialization or maturation effect?, *Social science & medicine, 24*(7), 619-624.

McCambridge, J., Witton, J., & Elbourne, D. R. (2014). Systematic review of the Hawthorne effect: new concepts are needed to study research participation effects. Journal of clinical epidemiology, 67(3), 267-277.

McDaniel, M. A., Anderson, J. L., Derbish, M. H., & Morrisette, N. (2007). Testing the testing effect in the classroom. *European Journal of Cognitive Psychology, 19*(4-5), 494-513.

Milkovich, G. T., Newman, J. M., & Milkovich, C. (1996). Compensation. Chicago: Irwin.

Risher, H., Fay, C. H., Holley, L. M., & O'Connell, J. R. (1997). New strategies for public pay: Rethinking government compensation programs. Jossey-Bass.

Schmidt, Frank & Hunter, John & McKenzie, Robert & Muldrow, Tressie. (1979). Impact of Valid Selection Procedures on Work-Force Productivity. Journal of Applied Psychology. 64. 609-626. 10.1037/0021-9010.64.6.609

Sekaran, U., & Bougie, R. (2016). Research methods for business: A skill building approach. John Wiley & Sons.

Setty, Prasad. "HR Meets Science at Google." *YouTube*, 10 Nov. 2014, www.youtube.com/watch?v=KY8v-O5Buyc.

Steers, R. M., & Rhodes, S. R. (1978). Major influences on employee attendance: A process model. Journal of applied Psychology, 63(4), 391.

Williams, R. (2003). Mellon learning curve research study. New York: Mellon Corp.

Made in the USA
Las Vegas, NV
20 December 2024

14776451R00122